laughing in the dark

A Comedian's
Journey through
Depression

laughing
in the dark

CHONDA PIERCE

HOWARD BOOKS
A DIVISION OF SIMON & SCHUSTER
New York   London   Toronto   Sydney

Howard Books, a division of Simon & Schuster, Inc.
1230 Avenue of the Americas, New York, NY 10020
www.howardpublishing.com

Laughing in the Dark © 2007 by Chonda Pierce

Library of Congress Cataloging-in-Publication Data TK

ISBN: 978-1-5011-1525-7

10 9 8 7 6 5 4 3 2 1

HOWARD colophon is a registered trademark of Simon & Schuster, Inc.

Manufactured in the United States of America

For information regarding special discounts for bulk purchases, please contact Simon & Schuster Special Sales at 1-800-456-6798 or business@simonandschuster.com.

Edited by Michele Buckingham
Cover design by John Lucas
Interior design by John Mark Luke Designs
Photography / illustrations by Michael Gomez

Special thanks to Vicki Graham, M.S.P.S., for providing the practical advice included in each chapter under the heading "Expert Insight."

The names on the emails to Chonda have been changed to protect the privacy of those who sent them, but each one is real and from Chonda's email inbox.

Unless otherwise noted, Scripture quotations marked NIV are taken from the Holy Bible, New International Version ®. Copyright © 1973, 1978, 1984 by International Bible Society. Used by permission of Zondervan. All rights reserved. Scripture quotations marked MSG are taken from The Message. Copyright © 1993, 1994, 1995, 1996, 2000, 2001, 2002. Used by permission of NavPress Publishing Group. Scripture quotations marked NASB are taken from the New American Standard Bible, © 1960, 1962, 1963, 1968, 1971, 1972, 1973, 1975, 1977 by The Lockman Foundation. Used by permission. Scripture quotations marked KJV are taken from the King James Version. Scripture quotations marked AMP are from the Amplified Bible®, copyright © 1954, 1958, 1962, 1964, 1965, 1987 by The Lockman Foundation. Used by permission (www.Lockman.org). Scriputre quotations marked TLB are from The Living Bible, copyright © 1971. Used by permission of Tyndale House Publishers, Inc., Wheaton, Illinois, 60189. Scripture quotatons marked NKJV are from the New King James Version®. Copyright © 1982 by Thomas Nelson, Inc. Used by permission. All rights reserved.

My deepest gratitude to my incredible family and friends
who refused to leave me alone in the dark.

This book is dedicated to anyone
sitting in the dark right now:

Hear me! You are never alone, my friend.

Fight the lies whispered in your ear today
and remember:

You will keep him in perfect peace,
Whose mind is stayed on You,
Because he trusts in You.

—Isaiah 26:3

Keep moving—even in the dark.
Your trust in Him will bring peace of mind.

Love,
Chonda

contents

contents

prologue

Without the assistance of that Divine Being…
I cannot succeed. With that assistance
I cannot fail. Trusting in Him who
can go with me, and remain with you,
and be everywhere for good, let us
confidently hope that all will yet be well.

—Abraham Lincoln

The God of all grace, who called

you to his eternal glory in Christ,

after you have suffered a little while,

will himself restore you and make

you strong, firm, and steadfast.

—1 Peter 5:10

my winter
break*down*

I think I know where Satan stays when he's on the road. You know, when he's hitting conventions and seminars and putting in personal appearances on movie sets. Or when he just wants to hang out with some of his zombie friends and needs a room with a pullout bed. Not long ago I stumbled across a place he'd probably call home. But then again, I was having a really bad day.

It was a hotel—one of a massive chain of hotels and motels with locations in every city, town, and neighborhood in America—that worked around the general theme of gray: gray walls, gray ceilings, gray floors. (Did I leave any surface out?) "Is a can of paint too much to ask?" I told the talking light when I passed by. That's right, a talking light. As I walked down the hallway toward the lobby, the beam lit up in dull gray and told me, "Watch your step." I looked down, but it was too late. I tripped over something gray and nearly broke my neck. A talking light! As my mom would say, "That's of the devil right there."

Let me describe this hotel to you. Perhaps you'll recognize it. You or someone you love may have been in one just like it. As I said, the walls, the ceilings, and the floors were gray. The lights talked—at least, when they wanted to. There was a big staircase up to the lobby, and on either side water cascaded down over a dark green light that shined up from somewhere below. I guess it was supposed to be an artistic kind of thing; but when I first saw the cascades, all I could think of was the green, slimy stuff from a scene in Ghostbusters. Other people milled through the lobby or lurked in dark corners, but I couldn't make out their faces; they were like gray, whispering shadows that never looked me in the eye.

Outside it was dark and gray and raining. Inside it was dark and gray and bubbling up green slime. I felt cold, gray, and alone. At any moment I expected the chandelier to announce, "God has left the building!"

But then again, did I tell you I was having a really bad day?

An Empty Tank

Winter break was over, and it was time for me to get back to work: back to airplane rides and sound checks, writing, performing, laughing, recording, more flights, more writing, more laughing, a bus tour, more performing, more laughing. Oh yeah—in case you don't know, I'm a comedian. Laughter is my job. If you don't laugh, I don't work. I'm also a wife and mother with a couple of teenaged children, a husband, three dogs, and a hamster. (At least, the hamster is alive at the time of this writing. By the time you read this . . . who knows? He has received a few threatening phone calls—that's all I'm going to say.)

During the winter I try to rest up and recharge. It's my time to kick back and enjoy my family and friends—to soak in some fun rather than dish it out. After a full spring, summer, and fall living at six laughs per minute, the winter is my personal time to refresh and refill the comedy tank.

But not this time. This time I spent my winter break in about four different hospitals, three clinics, six waiting rooms—not to mention an hour in that blood-pressure chair at the drugstore and multiple hours surfing between fourteen different Web sites that all begin with Medi-. My home base? The gray hotel with the talking lights and the green, bubbling slime. You see, this time instead of a winter break, I had a winter breakdown.

In the past I would have been rested, ready and itching to get back on the road. I love to make people laugh! But this time I wasn't sure how I was going to pull it off.

I don't want to sound like one of those VH-1 Behind-the-Scenes interviews, where the artist slobbers and snots all over herself complaining about how hard it will be to make the mortgage payment on the mansion this month, or how the oil in the Rolls Royce needs changing, or how, just when she gets all the bling-bling dusted, it's time to turn around and do it again. Have you seen that show? Seems as if everybody who's anybody has a rags-to-riches-to-rags story. Maybe a manager ran off with millions. Maybe a dysfunctional childhood haunts the person to this day. Maybe it all crumbled because of drugs or the inability to handle the stress and strain of life on the road.

Come to think of it—maybe I could do one of those episodes!

No, I'm just kidding. (See how that comedy thing works?) All my drugs were prescribed, my manager is great, and I have no bling-bling to brag about (let alone dust).

But other stories? Well, I have plenty of those. Trouble is . . . to share them with you, I'll have to take you on a journey through a few dark places.

Dark places in my childhood. Dark places in my heart and mind. Dark places in my not-always-six-laughs-per-minute life.

Get Me Out of Here!

On the kind of trip I've been on, you don't have to pack a thing. I've learned that the hard way. Besides, anything you might want to take along won't matter once you get there. You don't need a reservation. It's not one of those trips that you take—it takes you. And there's always room at the hotel.

Maybe you've already been there and back. If so, the territory I'm about to describe will seem familiar. You'll remember the gray walls, the whispering shadows, the dark corners, the places you just know Freddy Krueger is lurking—places you're sure God has abandoned. Maybe as we remember together, we'll find comfort in each other's company and rediscover the strength and the will to stay out of the dark.

Or maybe you just recently checked in to the hotel. Now you find yourself stuck in a place so gray and dreary and without joy that you wonder if you'll ever see the light of day again. I know how you feel. I've been there. So why not allow me to be your tour guide? Let me point out a few sights and sounds I'm familiar with. Let me tell you which doors to open, which hallways to avoid, and which dark corners are really not as mysterious as they seem. Together, let's look for the red glow of the EXIT light—the one that says, "This way out!"

I'm not a counselor, mind you. Like I said, I'm a comedian. But I've been to the hotel. I know 132 different shades of gray. I also know that life doesn't have to be gray forever. There was light at the end of my journey—and there is light at the end of yours too. So let's agree to stick together. Maybe we'll even have a laugh along the way.

Excuse me, but is that a talking lamp I hear? Or is it you—the one who's laughing in the dark?

chapter

1

What we receive by reaching our goals
is not nearly as important as what we
become while trying to reach them.

—Pastor Allen Jackson

Pity me, O Lord, for I am weak.

Heal me, for my body is sick, and I am

upset and disturbed. My mind is filled

with apprehension and with gloom.

Oh, restore me soon.

—Psalm 6:2–3 TLB

the big crash

In a very roundabout way, this journey begins in a remote, exotic setting on a small island off the coast of Mexico. And you know the saying: What happens in Mexico doesn't stay in Mexico. Or is it the other way around?

Anyway, there I was in Cozumel, Mexico, with my family just for the day. When you're on a cruise you can do that—hop off at a port in one country, spend the day buying monkey heads made out of coconut shells, hop to the next country, spend the day buying pocketbooks made from coconut shells, hop to the next and—well, you get the picture.

We were in Cozumel with a gaggle of other Christian

11

artists like Rebecca St. James, Mark Shultz, the guys and gals from FFH and Avalon, and various agents and promoters. Someone had the great idea that instead of shopping for coconut clothing, coconut furniture, and coconut lamps, we could ride mopeds across the island, have a quaint lunch at a secluded café—away from all the tourists—and then moped back.

"Wow!" my husband and children said. "That sounds like fun!"

Me? I had my heart set on the coconut salt and pepper shakers. But I got outvoted, and off we went on our rented mopeds.

The trip started out just like I'd imagine the brochure would promise (had there been a brochure). Sunny, sandy, tropical. A gorgeous shoreline that would take your breath away (but then again, so would an errant bug down the windpipe). What no one told us, however—and the reason there probably was no brochure—is that for most of the trip, we were going to have to share the road with all the normal traffic. All the normal, speeding traffic.

Jeff Allen is a fellow comedian who hates to shop, so he'd talked his wife into the moped jaunt (is that the right word?). At the halfway point she careened into a ravine and nearly broke her leg. Another woman did—break her leg, that is. And another woman, one who was putt-putt-putting along just ahead of me, simply drove off into the swamp. It was like she never even tried to turn. I was afraid I'd just witnessed suicide-by-moped.

My husband and son stopped and helped pull her out of the muck. She was scratched up a bit, but otherwise fine. I still don't know her name. To this day I call her "the-lady-who-almost-died-on-a-moped." But then, there is a busload of people who probably know me only by that name as well. Yes, I too nearly got creamed on a moped.

Mopeds are strange animals. Ours were so old and rickety that you had to aim to the left to make the front wheels go in a straight line. Therefore, a right-hand turn was almost impossible. I know because I risked it. And I risked it because a city bus was coming at me head-on. I needed to turn and turn fast. I'd take a swamp over a city bus any day!

Now, I was no stranger to "the hog." I'd driven a motorcycle in high school. I know what it feels like to hop on 80cc's of raw power. I'd also learned in high school (besides the fact that it's totally impossible to miss a chicken that decides to cross the road in front of you) that if you jerk the front wheel of a motorcycle with all your might, something will happen.

So I turned hard, just as I felt city-bus metal brush against the sleeve of my jacket. So this is how it ends, I remember thinking. Smashed by the Ocho Nueve in Cozumel, Mexico. (That's Bus Number 89 for those of you who don't speak Spanish. And for those of you who do, I won't repeat what I heard coming from the people inside the bus.)

I yanked the moped onto the grass and came to a dusty halt. And then I cried. Hard. When I finished, I slowly putt-putted myself back to town and spent the rest of the day buying coconut souvenirs for people I hadn't thought about in years. A near-death experience will do that to you.

So thanks to my motorcycle expertise and, no doubt, a whole host of guardian angels, I avoided a nasty crash in a faraway land. What I didn't know at the time was that wiping out on a moped in Cozumel was a breeze compared to the big crash that awaited me in Miami a couple of weeks later.

I told you my almost-got-killed-on-a-moped story so that when I explain how I left the cruise ship (it was work, mind you), raced home, did some laundry, and headed back out to a swanky hotel and spa in Miami, you won't hate me. The Miami thing had been planned for a while. You see, I'd held a contest months earlier for my Turbo Host of the Year. (The contestants were the volunteers who helped organize my concerts in each of the towns I visited.) The winner was a sweet young woman named Melanie. The prize? My girlfriends and I took her to be pampered, because that's what girlfriends do when there's a trip to a spa in Miami on the schedule! We chose Super Bowl Sunday for our trip because we knew there'd be no pampering at home; most of our husbands would be too engrossed in the Big Game.

So this is how it ends, smashed by the Ocho Nueve in Cozumel, Mexico.

I was especially tired that weekend. And I had an upset stomach—but hey, I had almost been killed in Mexico. Which was another reason to sign up for the Pamper Package: massage, facial, pedicure, manicure, and half a dozen other things that end in cure or massage.

Our luxurious beachside accommodations were on the fifteenth floor of the hotel, overlooking the beautiful Atlantic. The little soaps and shampoos in the basket in the bathroom were some kind of high-class rosemary mint stuff—not your generic soap bars that never lather. Not here! Every liquid or gel at this place had a bit of "oo-la-la" mixed in—the oils and the perfumes and the moisturizers and even the shoe polish. I didn't want to miss a single amenity. I tried a dab of every bottle, tube, bar, and squeeze pack in the place. (It gave me the same kind of excited feeling I used to get as a kid whenever the government cheese truck would roll through the neighborhood.) I used it all and smelled like a bouquet. Then I washed most of it off, scrubbing especially hard to remove the shoe polish from my wrists and behind my ears.

And then there was the spa! That first day we plopped into the hot tub, cooked in the sauna, and boiled in the Jacuzzi. We didn't miss a single body of water. I'm not sure if we were supposed to soak in that cute fountain thing in the foyer or not. (Don't worry, we didn't.) What made it all even better was that back home in Tennessee, it was snowing. Could we have asked for a more perfect weekend?

Well, maybe perfect isn't the best word. Like I told you, there was a big crash coming; I just didn't know it. And if you haven't guessed yet, it took place in mid-spa . . .

Where Are the Pillow Mints?

Late Saturday night, nearly two days into our fancy-schmancy pampering weekend, I got a sharp pain in my chest, and I couldn't take a deep breath. "That's okay," one of my friends said. "Just take lots of little breaths." That sounded like good, solid math to me. So I did. I took lots of short, shallow breaths, while my heart raced and panic tried to creep in.

"I know what we can do," someone else said. "Let's go to a fancy restaurant." And so we did, because that's what girlfriends do when they're on a fancy-schmancy pampering weekend. And that seemed to take care of the problem—at least for a while.

The next morning I was still having a hard time breathing. I wondered if I was allergic to shoe polish. My girlfriends tried to get to the root of the problem. Someone started a list. Was it the Italian food from the night before? No it started before that. What about the donuts? No, donuts love me. The little mints on the pillows? ("Those were mints, weren't they, girls?" I remember asking.) How about the bag of bagels from the Mexican restaurant across the street? (I know, bagels at a Mexican restaurant? Don't ask!)

Meanwhile, someone fired up the laptop and began surfing the Internet. We had seaweed wraps and moon-rock massages lined up for the afternoon, so we had to find a cure quick. You know, I have a feeling the Internet will soon be the number one "reason to see a doctor." Somewhere between beyourowndoctor.com and homeremedies-R-us.net (they're not real Web site names, but they'd be great ones, don't you think?), a girl could get killed. I sat on the couch, barely breathing, while the Spa Brigade asked me a battery of questions. After each question someone would move the mouse, and I'd hear a click. After about twenty minutes of pointing and clicking, my friends determined that either (1) I was having a heart attack, (2) I had developed a gallstone, or (3) I needed a lung transplant.

After two more point-and-clicks, someone offered another possibility. "Could be that you just crashed into menopause," she said. If it weren't for the fact that I couldn't breathe already, that would have taken my breath away. "You mean, I'm not going to be able to breathe again until I'm sixty-five?"

Another sharp pain hit me in the chest, and I began to feel faint. I fell back deeper into the sofa. The plush

> "Could be that you just crashed into menopause," she said. If it weren't for the fact that I couldn't breathe already, that would have taken my breath away.

cushions of the fancy-schmancy hotel felt nice, but the pain in my chest was killing me. I prayed for gallstones.

One of the girls on our trip was my friend Alison. I call her Alison the Angel now. She's known me since before high school. She's seen me when I've been healthy and happy and when I've been tired and ill. She's seen me when I've been cranky and irritable and when I've been happy-go-lucky. She's even seen me skinny—that's how far back we go. But she'd never seen me clutch my chest and fall back on a sofa.

"Okay, that's it," she said, moving to the center of the room and pointing a hairbrush as if she were a conductor with a baton. "Nicole, call the front desk and get a cab. Melanie, get Chonda's purse and find her driver's license and medical card. Michelle, dig out the Yellow Pages and find the nearest emergency room."

Everything was a blur after that—that is, until we got to the emergency room. Then everything turned into a slow crawl. I waited for a few hours before finally settling into a bed in the ER (no pillow mints). I waited some more, and then someone wheeled me to x-ray so the doctors could get a look at my lungs. At some point I had an EKG, and a number of times the nurses showed up to draw blood. They told me that each new vial was for a different test, and all the tests had letters for names: BMP, QLT, ABC, and LMNOP. I figured the last test would tell them that I was a little low on blood.

At one point a nurse came by and said, "The doctors want to keep you overnight and run more tests." My imagination kicked in, and I pictured a group of hurried and harried doctors gathering in the hall just out of earshot and taking a vote:

"What do you think we ought to do with Chonda?"

"I say we keep her overnight."

"Yeah, that way we can take more blood and run more tests. There are still lots of letters in the alphabet. But we're definitely going to need more needles."

The nurse tried to comfort me by promising me a bed upstairs in a private room as soon as it became available. "With little soaps and oils?" I asked. She looked at me, as if maybe I were joking. I get that all the time.

Apparently the bed never came open, because I stayed in the emergency room the rest of that day, all night, and most of the next morning. Alison never left my side. The other girls kept vigil too. When Monday came, however, the Spa Brigade had to head for the airport, because most of them had real jobs to get back to. The longer I was in the ER, it seemed, the more I was running out of company—and blood.

Just when I was beginning to feel really sorry for myself, my husband, David, came walking in. If ever there was time for theme music to start playing, that was it! David had never been to Miami in his life; but he and Ken, Alison's husband, had been scuba diving that weekend in the Dominican Republic and happened to be changing planes in Miami. (They may have been the only two men in America who had chosen not to devote the weekend to football.) Knowing that I was in the city somewhere, he called my cell phone. Alison answered, and when she told him what had been going on, he hopped in a cab and came straight to the hospital. In no time at all he was playing Twenty Questions with the doctors.

One doctor thought there could be a problem with my lungs, so he gave me a pill that was supposed to relax my breathing. Another doctor was suspicious of the soaps and oils at the spa, so he ordered allergy tests. Another wanted to know more about the trip I'd taken to Mexico a couple of weeks earlier—if I'd touched any farm animals, things like that. Part of me was afraid I had a strange and rare disease, maybe the first case ever; and from then on it would simply be known as the Chonda Disease, which would mean doctors all over the world would be in search of the Chonda vaccine. That couldn't be good for a career in comedy.

By this time I was so tired and weak, all I really wanted to do was go home. After convincing the kind ER doctor that this was a good idea (it wasn't easy, because his accent was strong, and my Spanish is pathetic—I was worried that what little Spanish I did know was sounding like the phrases I'd heard coming from the bus windows back in Cozumel), I collected my things and headed for the airport with David.

Pills, Pastors, and a Hot Shower

I slept through most of the flight home and vaguely remember crawling into my bed. Two days passed and all I could manage to do was sleep. Each time I woke, I planned to take a hot shower, have a bite to eat, and snap out of it.

Six weeks later I finally took that shower. I'm certain I took a bath—or washed my face, at least—in the meantime. But only after six weeks, three hospital stays, four trips to the emergency room, three pastoral visits (four, if you count a Billy Graham Crusade rerun from 1974), seventeen prescriptions, and every diagnostic test known to man, was I finally able to stand for a few minutes under the warm flow of water without falling apart.

In those six weeks the doctors considered every possible diagnosis, from an inner ear infection to leukemia, from intestinal parasites to a bleeding ulcer—and I had all the medicines on my coffee table to prove it. I had an antibiotic just in case I had picked up something in Mexico, another drug just in case I was experiencing vertigo, a steroid of some sort that the doctor told me "ought to kill just about anything you've got," and a decongestant just in case my nagging cough got worse.

In other words, I had a lot of drugs given to me "just in case." I washed down the pills like clockwork with cans of Ensure, because food was not doing it for me.

But instead of getting stronger, all I wanted to do was sleep—or cry. I wanted to hang onto things—solid things like the sofa, the coffee table, the door jamb—anything to keep

> Each time I woke, I planned to take a hot shower, have a bite to eat, and snap out of it. Six weeks later I finally took that shower.

me from spinning into the strong downward spiral that seemed to be tugging at me with all its might.

I called my pastor and his wife twelve times. They came over four. That last time, when I was still not feeling any better, I figured I needed something more than your average prayer. I told Pastor Allen that I needed deliverance.

"From what?" he asked.

"I don't know," I said. "Must be something I can't remember. Don't you have a prayer for that?"

So we prayed. But it didn't work. At least not the way I had imagined it would—you know, with a burst of light, a rumble, maybe a loud, clashing cymbal or two. My apologies to Pastor Allen, but I was afraid that maybe he just wasn't connected. So I asked others over, searching for the one devout soul whose prayers could reach heaven. I had the Bible-study ladies over, my mother, my brother, my sister-in-law, my cousins—I even asked my husband to flag down the mailman and try to determine what sort of spiritual fellow he was, if at all. I was desperate to hear from God!

That evening Pastor Allen came back, this time with Dr. Wayne Westmoreland, a prominent surgeon in our community. A surgeon! So it's come to this, I thought. Dr. Wayne has a kind smile, and that evening he sat on the edge of the couch where I had been crashed for weeks and pressed and poked around my stomach. The Ensure sloshed with each poke.

"What do you think?" I asked him.

He pursed his lips and said, "I'm a surgeon. So I'm looking for something I can cut out."

"Take what you need, Doc," I said. Couldn't be worse!

The truth was, Dr. Wayne was in a better position to evaluate my condition than anyone else at that point. Each emergency room visit over the previous six weeks had resulted in one more doctor adding one more medicine to battle one more symptom. By the time Dr. Wayne found me on the sofa sloshing with Ensure, I was smack-dab in the middle of one nasty fight. I had lost fifteen pounds (now there's a silver lining for you!), and I was so severely dehydrated that I don't think I could have worked up a good spit if I'd wanted to. Pinch my skin, and it stood straight up. Every tear was a miracle.

After more poking and prodding, Dr. Wayne said, "First, let's pray." Then, over the next few moments, he asked the Lord for healing, for wisdom, and for direction. These were probably the most soothing moments I had experienced in weeks. When the prayer was over, he looked at the bottles of medicines on the coffee table next to me and said, "First of all, we can cut this out." He waved his surgeon's hand over the prescriptions and said, "Let's start all over, Chonda. Let's get all the drugs out of your system and begin again. Your body has failed you. Your system has taken a jolt, and we need to find out why. We've got to get you back on your feet."

Then, with tears in his eyes, he said, "You make too many people laugh to be lying here any longer."

At that, I sobbed—which made him cry too. Not the kind of response I'm used to. I'm a comedian, remember?

A Bad Knock-Knock Joke

Because I passed out at some point the next day, I went back to the emergency room. My girlfriend, Alison, had flown in from her home in South Carolina to relieve Doris, my sister-in-law, who had been with me nonstop for three weeks. Alison and David packed me into the car, and I found myself for a fifth time looking up at all the familiar faces in the ER. I tried to smile whenever I could.

The IV that pumped fluids into my system made me feel better physically, but an overwhelming sense of darkness seemed to hang over me, like a low ceiling that was cold and poorly lit. I met a really nice specialist, who poked and prodded my stomach a few more times and then listened to my insides with his stethoscope. "I've never heard intestines talk so much," he commented.

My sweet husband, standing at my side, took my hand and said, "Is that what they mean by 'inside voice'?"

The doctor told me that he wanted to put a camera down my throat and take a video of what was going on in there. It would be the first video I'd ever done without having to worry about buying a new outfit. A nurse came by a few minutes later and gave me a shot that made the gurney ride back to Surgery as fun as a Disney World ride. I swallowed the camera, and in a few minutes the video was complete. And shortly after that, the doctor had a diagnosis: "Looks like you have a hiatal hernia."

> An overwhelming sense of darkness seemed to hang over me, like a low ceiling that was cold and poorly lit.

"That's it?" I said.

"Well, that's one thing," he said. "Honestly? We may never know how you got to this point—what made you so physically sick. By the time you got here, you had so many different medications in your system that your esophagus and tummy had had enough. Frankly, your insides are a nervous wreck."

He wrote me prescriptions for Nexium and Zelnorm. I knew what they were because I'd seen the commercials on TV. I knew they would soothe my nervous insides. Then he wrote another prescription for Zoloft. I hadn't heard of that one. "What's this one for?" I asked.

"Depression," he said, as if he answered that question

every day. "You are depressed. This will help until you get back on your feet."

Me, depressed? But I'm a comedian. "How long do I have to take it?"

He shrugged. "I don't know. Maybe six months. Maybe a year."

But I have to get back to work! I have jokes to write. How can I write a joke when I'm depressed? Will it sound like this: "Knock-knock. Go away!"?

"Or you may have to take it the rest of your life," he added—as if that would be a routine thing. "I'm also going to recommend that you see a therapist or counselor. That'll do wonders for your insides too."

He had barely left the room when, what did I do? I told Alison to call her husband, Ken. Did I mention Ken is a doctor?

"Ken will set things straight," I told her. "No way do I need Zoloft! I'll be fine. It's just a bad case of heartburn. A supreme pizza makes me feel the same way."

But Alison had that look on her face. Alison, my friend of twenty-five years who—did I mention?—also happens to have a doctorate in psychology, who also happens to chair the Mental Health Commission for the State of South Carolina, was giving me her look. It's the expression she uses whenever she thinks someone is wrong: she tilts her head to one side, flashes her eyes, and draws her lips tight and thin.

Alison knows all about Zoloft. So she took the time to tell me about it. She also told me about serotonin—the stuff manufactured somewhere in the brain that's supposed to flow into your central nervous system and tell the body that everything's just fine. Too much serotonin, and you can get stuck in laugh-mode. Too little, and you can slip into depression.

Yes, Alison knows all about Zoloft. More than once she even used it and the word miracle in the same sentence.

As I listened to what she had to say, my "inside voice" reluctantly concurred. Alison and the doctor were right. I was depressed. Deeply, darkly depressed. My world had been losing color for weeks, if not months. Now I was living in a thick, cold grayness that seemed to have no end.

I folded the little white prescription notes in half and handed them to my husband.

"Here, honey," I said. "Better get these filled."

To: Chonda
Subject: Thank you!
From: Debbie

Dear Chonda,

I have suffered with clinical depression for years. I didn't believe it could get better or come to an end. You gave me hope and helped me understand that I didn't cause this horrible cloud of gloom. Thank you for all you do to make the road a little easier for the rest of us.

Debbie

expert
insight

Vicki Graham has a fancy degree in Master of Science and Psychological Service, which has allowed her to practice as a psychotherapist for fifteen years and serve as a consultant to law enforcement agencies as an expert witness for the courts. Now she shares her education and gifts through her writing; and we are honored to be blessed by her expert, practical advice in each chapter of this book.

Know the Symptoms

Most psychotherapists and clinicians agree that the number one problem in treating patients with depression is denial. The patient doesn't feel well, but she'd rather not think the problem may be psychological. So she seeks the help of a medical physician. The physician, who isn't trained in the psychological or psychiatric fields, diagnoses and medicates for physical symptoms. When the patient doesn't improve (or worsens), her sense of hopelessness increases—and so does her depression.

Honesty about your mental state is the best route to take if you're suffering with depression symptoms. Answer the following questions to see if clinical depression may be an issue in your life:

1. Are you experiencing melancholy moods or the loss of pleasure?

2. Are you sad most of the time?

3. Have you had a change in appetite?

4. Have you lost or gained weight recently?

5. Do you have trouble sleeping or want to sleep most of the time?

6. Do you feel fatigued or have very low energy?

7. Do you have low self-esteem or feelings of hopelessness?

8. Do you have feelings of worthlessness or inappropriate guilt?

9. Do you have difficulty thinking or concentrating?

10. Do you have morbid or suicidal thoughts?

If you answered "yes" to at least five of these questions and your symptoms have lasted more than two weeks, then a depression disorder may exist, according to the American Psychiatric Association's Diagnostic and Statistical Manual of Mental Disorders, Fourth Edition, virtually the bible of mental-health clinicians and psychotherapists.

For examples and more details about depression symptoms, check the Web site www.depression.com. If you suspect that you are depressed, see a qualified mental-health specialist who can accurately pinpoint a diagnosis, perhaps administer tests and, if appropriate, prescribe an antidepressant medication that will help get you on the road to recovery.

chapter

2

Having a depressed person in the family
is like having a death in the family.
At least the dead person has the
decency to not be around anymore.

—David Feherty

Hear my cry, O God; listen to my prayer.

From the ends of the earth I call to you,

I call as my heart grows faint.

Lead me to the rock that is higher than I.

—Psalm 61:1–2

not so well
with my soul

The thing about taking those little blue pills that are supposed to lift you from the dumps is that they don't work right away. I pictured them working the way nitroglycerin pills work for heart patients. You know, you've seen the TV shows: The man falls on the floor and crawls his way to the coffee table, where he left his pill bottle. He claws off the cap, spills most of the little buggers, then picks one out of the shag carpet and pokes it under his tongue just as he is about to pass out. In two seconds, he's breathing better. In three, he's smiling. In five, he's cleaning up his mess and fussing about the child-proof cap. Now that's fast. And that's what I wanted. But my pills didn't work like that.

chapter 2

"It'll take about two weeks before you start noticing any change in the way you feel," the doctor told me.

What?

"And about four weeks before there's enough medicine in your system to make you feel well consistently. Until then you may experience waves of up and down."

"You mean, an emotional roller coaster?"

"Yeah, something like that."

I called the doctor and asked him (for the one-hundred-twelfth time) if he had a faster pill. He said no.

I'd been on emotional roller coasters before. I have two nearly grown children. It's amazing how many ups and downs teenagers can go through, not to mention their mothers. But those fluctuations were nothing compared to what I was experiencing now. This new roller coaster made the Beast—that monster ride at King's Island in Ohio—look like a puppy.

I'm not big on patience. If a meal takes longer than five minutes in the microwave, I usually outsource it. So what did I do? I went to Disney World.

Well, not exactly. I did go to Orlando, because that's

where my brother, Mike, was pastoring a church at the time. Technically, that put me in the same neighborhood as Mickey.

Numb and Numb-er

I tried to stay home and wait for the medicines to kick in—I really did. The doctor told me to rest and eat well so that my body could get stronger physically. Rest? I'd been in bed (or on the sofa or on a hospital gurney) for the last six weeks. I was tired of resting. But I was also very weak. The doctor was right: I needed to regain my strength. Unfortunately, all I could eat was applesauce.

"Then eat lots of it," he said, "and drink Ensure—something with vitamins and protein."

My kids took me on walks. Made sure I didn't fall down. Told me what was going on in the news. Tried to make me laugh. But the fact that they were treating me like I remembered treating my ninety-five-year-old grandmother just depressed me more. I called the doctor and asked him (for the one-hundred-twelfth time) if he had a faster pill. He said no. I told him I'd pay cash, that there'd be no hassles with insurance forms, co-pays, or anything like that. He told me a faster pill doesn't exist. "Just be patient."

I went back to the sofa and watched my husband paint the living room. "This ought to cheer you up," he said. I didn't have the heart to tell him that taupe is not a cheery color. He was trying.

Doris, my sister-in-law, came up from Orlando for a second visit. Doris is kind and meek and soft-spoken, and she has a really nice reading voice. I made her read me the Psalms one after another. In the past, the Psalms had always been a surefire way to lift my spirits. This time—nothing. Nada. Why couldn't I feel anything? Why couldn't I rejoice when David rejoiced on his harp? Why didn't the blaring of the trumpets or the loud, clanging cymbals move me? My emotions were so numb, it was as if an Out of Order sign had been thumbtacked across my heart. Instead of dancing with the ancient king, I sank deeper into the sofa.

Doris hung in there with me for a couple of weeks and read so much that she almost went hoarse. She was definitely in danger of losing her nice reading voice. I still felt nothing. And February is such a dreary month in Tennessee anyway. In fact, we were on pace to set some sort of local record for rainfall. In the previous twenty-one days, it had rained eighteen. I was bluer than the pills I was taking—pills that didn't seem to be working at all!

Finally sweet, soft-spoken Doris had had enough. "We're going to Florida!" she said, kind of raspy-like.

But then there was the hassle of plane tickets and airports and all. The thought of flying somewhere—even somewhere sunny—was overwhelming. That's when I called my manager and said, "Can you make the bus come pick me up and take me to Florida?" Maybe I cried a little. All I know is that in a couple of hours, the bus was at my door. The driver who'd taken care of me for so many miles and so many long hours on the road stepped out into the rain to help with the bags. Phil is a gentle giant—and a great cook. When I climbed into the bus (in my housecoat and slippers) the aroma of Phil's famous roast beef casserole enveloped me, and I never wanted anther bite of applesauce again. Doris and I settled in on the bus, and Phil asked if I needed anything else.

My emotions were so numb, it was as if an Out of Order sign had been thumbtacked across my heart.

"A fork," I told him.

David stayed behind because the new carpet was coming later that week. I didn't have the heart to tell him that Berber is not a cheery kind of carpet at all. He was doing the best he could.

My husband has always had enough patience for both of us. This time I had to have patience of my own. This was my battle to wage. David, God bless him, thought it might help if I waged it in a freshly painted room with new carpet. I didn't want to burst his bubble by telling him that redecorating probably wouldn't make much difference. In the frame of mind I was in, even bright yellow and chartreuse would have seemed like variations of gray.

Twelve hours after Phil showed up, our bus rolled into Orlando, where it was sunny and warm. Who could be depressed when it's sunny and warm in February? Me! I think I had half-expected to just "snap out of it" when I saw my brother Mike or when I felt the warm Florida sunshine on my face or when I smelled the summery aroma of fresh-cut grass or when I got to eat ice cream outside on the patio—in February. Nope.

For the next five or six days, Mike took Doris's place as primary reader. He read from Matthew and Luke and John, from Proverbs and Isaiah. He even read a short passage from Habakkuk, just to see if that might be the one holy combination of Scripture verses that would break me out of my grayness. Nothing doing.

We tried singing. Mike, Doris, and I gathered around the piano; and with each old hymn or worship song we sang, I tried to convince myself that it was, indeed, "well with my soul." But it that were true, then why couldn't I feel something—anything?

Movie R_x

Finally I had a breakthrough.

Mike had planned for his whole church to go as a group to watch the opening of the Mel Gibson movie The Passion of the Christ. It was a big event for congregations all across the country that winter. Mike and Doris wanted me to go too.

I'd already seen the film once, before my big crash. I'd been invited to a preview screening, along with some country-music folks from Nashville. Now, as I considered seeing the film again, I remembered back to the wide range of emotions I'd felt at the preview—sadness, guilt, appreciation, unworthiness, the sheer joy of my salvation. I'd sobbed and sobbed. Mel Gibson had even shown up in person. Talk about an emotional roller coaster! It had thrilled my soul to hear this big Hollywood movie star say that he believes Jesus is coming back again (only this time he's going to be pretty ticked off). That had really fired me up.

Maybelcouldgetthatbackagain—allthoseemotions—at the theater.

And so I went to see The Passion with my temporary church family in Florida. I sat close to the back, beneath a glowing Exit light, so that I would have less walking to do coming in and going out. The first time I'd seen the film, I'd been healthy and well. This time, I was broken and weak and frail and lost. I came from a whole different vantage point.

For a second time, I watched the on-screen portrayal of our Savior, who was broken and beaten and mocked, yet remained strong—for us, for his children. For me. I didn't just pray that night. I tried—bathed in the light that radiated from the final scene of the movie—to believe: Surely his sacrifice was more than enough for my problem. After all, his power overcame the grave! All I had was a hiatal hernia (and the video to prove it). Should be a piece of cake for him, I figured.

> Surely his sacrifice was more than enough for my problem. After all, his power overcame the grave! Should be a piece of cake for him, I figured.

My confidence began to grow that night. I knew my stomach problems would be healed. Maybe not instantly. There'd be no stopping for hot wings on the way home from the movie, but that was okay. I knew my tummy would be fine in time. I could just feel it.

Finally I could feel something!

What I wasn't quite as aware of, though, was that a bigger battle was being waged within me. And the battleground was not restricted to my stomach.

Who would have guessed that in this little brain of mine, there'd be so much room for me to get so lost? And not a single Exit light to be found!

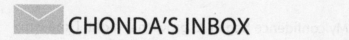

CHONDA'S INBOX

To:	Chonda
Subject:	Thank you for sharing
From:	Gina

Dear Chonda,

Thank you, thank you, thank you! I just returned home from the Women of Faith conference, and what a joyful weekend it was! Your description of how depression feels hit home. I've experienced depression off and on for five years. I have been through counseling, medication, friends' good intentions, etc. But knowing that I'm not alone gives me the hope I need the most! Thank you for sharing your life with the rest of us and allowing us to laugh with you.

Gina

expert insight

What Friends Can—and Can't—Do to Help

Friends can be a great help in a depressed person's recovery. When a woman is depressed, her friends, by their very presence, can remind her that she is not alone. They can let her know that she is loved. On a practical level, they can help relieve some of her stress by volunteering to run a few errands, do a load of laundry, or watch her kids for a day.

On the other hand, friends can sometimes interfere in a depressed person's progress toward healing. They may mean well and have the patient's best interests at heart; but if they don't understand depression or if they have strong opinions about psychotherapy or medication, their advice and attention can be detrimental. Some psychotherapists go so far as to forbid their patients to talk about their cases to friends or relatives.

If you have a friend who is clinically depressed, the best things you can do for her are to pray for her, encourage her to follow her doctor's orders, support her in her efforts to get well, and give her a degree of privacy when it comes to her illness. Don't try to "fix" her, push her to talk, or bombard her with your "expert" opinions. Instead, give her room so that she doesn't feel as if she's under a microscope—as if you're taking note of every minor improvement or temporary failure in her progress toward healing. Give her space without backing out of her life. She doesn't need another doctor or therapist, and she definitely doesn't need more pressure from the people around her. She simply needs a friend who loves her, who will stand beside her, and who has the faith to believe that she will get well.

chapter
3

A ship in harbor is safe,
but that is not what
ships are built for.

—John A. Shedd

A good man asks advice from friends;

the wicked plunge ahead—and fall.

—Proverbs 12:26 MSG

rehearse in the dark what you learned in the light

After about four months my general practitioner said he didn't see any reason why I couldn't go back to work. "Just take it easy," he said.

Or maybe it was the mortgage company that broke the news.

In any case, I immediately called Alison in South Carolina and asked her what she thought about the idea of me touring again. (It's always nice when a reliable second opinion is just a phone call away!) She was in her office, so I got her "professional voice."

"Well, how do you feel about going back to work?" she asked.

Frankly, I hated the idea. The last thing I felt like doing was going on the road and earning a living by trying to make people laugh. I wasn't sure I had any "funny" left in me.

"I don't think I can do it anymore," I said.

"Of course you can," Alison responded.

I wasn't sure whether she was speaking as a professional or as a girlfriend. I do know that I leaned on Alison and my husband, David, to always shoot straight with me. Within hours the two of them were on the phone with my manager, my agent—and together they decided which events would be the least taxing. As the plans developed, David and Alison kept rooting me on. "Make your body tell your brain who's in charge," they encouraged me. To this day I'm not sure that either of them were 100 percent certain I could get back on stage. But they cheered for me as if I were about to enter a boxing ring for the championship title!

And the truth was, that's how it felt to me. Work at that point seemed very much like stepping into a boxing ring. Do you know how hard it is to nail a punch line? To slay an audience? Or, on bad nights, to totally flop? Comedy can be exhausting—not to mention packing the suitcase and catching the airplane and waiting in the hotel lobby for the ride that gets you to the venue three hours early so you can read old church bulletins, because there's nothing else to do until the show begins. And then there's the racing back to the hotel afterwards, trying to get there before room service shuts down, so you're not stuck with whatever you can get out of the vending machine at the end of the hallway (provided you have the right change).

But ready or not, the arrangements were made, and the boxing match was on. Before I left town, I promised the doctor I'd take it easy. At least, I'd try to get a room next to the vending machine.

Road Warriors

Lucky for me I travel with Mary and Martha.

I told you my sister-in-law's name is Doris. But really it's Mary. She's sweet and tender. When I want to cry, she'll cry with me—real tears. She'll hold me and say things like, "There, there now. Just let it all go. Everything's going to be all right." She'll comfort me and take care of me. She is my nurturer. Whatever I need to eat—whether it's a spoonful of applesauce or a verse from the Word—she'll provide it. She'll warm me up a bowl of chicken noodle soup or break open the latest Beth Moore Bible study. When I want to laugh, she'll guffaw—again, real tears. She'll snort and turn red-faced as if she's just heard the funniest thing ever. I get a peaceful, easy feeling whenever Mary—I mean, Doris—is in the room.

And then there's Martha—I mean Alison, my best friend, the one who got me to the hospital in Miami when I had my big crash. She has a way of bursting into a room and taking control. For instance, if I'm curled up on the floor crying, and Doris is hanging over me and stroking my hair and snotting and crying along, Alison will say, "Get me a cold wash rag." Then, after she cleans off my face (she makes Doris wipe her own nose), she'll say something like, "You have to get dressed, because it's time to go to work." It's a tough job, but someone has to do it. And Martha—I mean, Alison—is good at it. She has a degree in that kind of work.

The Mary-and-Martha routine was exactly what was going on my first day back at work. The three of us were sitting on the floor of the "green room" (for all of you non-show-biz types, that's the waiting room before you go on stage). At least, Alison and Doris were sitting. I was laid out—"hugging the carpet," as they say. I didn't want to go on stage. I didn't think I could go on stage.

This was no small-time event—the kind where I could say, "Excuse me," and someone would step in, sing a special, and skip over my part. This was a kick-off session of a major Women of Faith conference. About twenty-thousand women were gathered for the day, and I was the one they hired to be funny. Alison reminded me of that again. Twenty-thousand women...have to be funny. I heard her just fine with one ear. My other ear was mashed too hard against the carpet to hear anything other than the constant footfalls of other guests coming in and out of the green room.

Alison gently wiped a cool rag across my face. "You just have to do what you know how to do," she told me. "Just do what you do. The rest will follow."

My mind began to race with all sorts of thoughts: What if I pass out in front of twenty-thousand women? How embarrassing would that be? What if my outfit isn't cool? Do I have any zits? (No, if I did, Alison would have told me.) What if I'm not funny? What if I just don't "have it" anymore? What will I do? What will my family do? Chera

> "Just do what you do. The rest will follow."

wants to go to med school! Where is Zachary's report card? What kind of wife am I? David has to iron his own shirts!

Is this carpet Berber? Why does this room look so dull and

gray? Did that light just say something? I miss my sisters. Why won't God heal me? I can't be seen like this. I'm supposed to be joyful! My lips are chapped. What if I forget a punch line? Go away, Martha. I want my Mary!

Somehow I eventually got up off the carpet. Mary and Martha straightened me up. They prayed with me. Alison pointed me toward the stage, and the three of us walked in that general direction. I heard a disembodied voice talking about me, and in a couple of seconds I realized it was coming from the sound system. Someone was introducing me to the audience. I heard a cheer and felt the familiar cool metal of the microphone slide into my hand.

"Just do what you do," Alison whispered.

I looked over at Doris, and she smiled. I could tell that she wanted to throw her arms around me. I could feel her love, if not her hug—and that was enough.

I stepped onto the stage. The lights were bright and shined directly into my eyes, so that I couldn't see any faces. Beyond the glare, everything was dark. I opened my mouth and said something funny—at least I think I did, because I heard a roar of laughter coming from the darkness. Each laugh became a bridge to the next one. I was familiar with this route; I'd taken it thousands of times. So I traveled it again this night. I worked the only way I knew how—but not by any strength of my own, of that I'm sure.

I pushed through my twenty-five minute monologue and ended with the song "God Loves You." I had used this material before, and it had always worked in the past. I didn't trust myself to veer from the script; I knew I was in no shape to talk about the things that were swirling in my head. "Rehearse in the dark what you learned in the light"—that's a saying I repeat often these days.

Everything seemed to go well. I told jokes. The audience laughed. I sang. The audience clapped. But as soon as I stepped off the stage, released the microphone, and felt Doris loop an arm through mine and lead me away from the lights, I began to cry.

When I reached the green room, Alison was there with another wet cloth. I wanted to fall down on the rug and cry, but Alison wouldn't have it. She pointed me to a chair. Reluctantly I plopped into the seat, like a boxer crashing into his corner after making it through Round 12. My fight managers immediately began encouraging me and patching me up.

"You did great," Doris said.

"We'll go back to the hotel and rest up," Alison added.

"Then tomorrow we'll come back and do this again. Just once more."

You mean, I'm going to have to tell more jokes? I wanted to throw in the towel; but then, I'd have to wrestle it away from Alison first, and I was pretty sure I couldn't do that. So I said, "Doris, read me something from the Psalms again." Doris smiled, opened her Bible, and began to read, while I cried some more. Alison caught my tears with the cool washcloth. She knew I hadn't packed another outfit, and the one I was wearing was dry clean only.

Balancing Act

Those early days back at work are still a bit of a blur. But somehow I made it through. The key, I discovered, was having good friendships—and having them in the right balance. Start with a heaping helping of Mary, throw in a few cupfuls of Martha, and almost anything is possible!

Having Doris and Alison in my corner may not seem like much to you—but to me? Well, I'm still amazed to think that long before I ever slipped into this dark ring, God was already putting my fight team in place. That means one thing: He knew I would be there. He knew I would need loyal, devoted friends who would help me protect with my right, jab with my left, float like a butterfly, sting like a bee . . .

Depression has many signs. It's a complicated battle. And while you can find lots of good (and bad) information on the Internet, your best resource is your doctor if you think you might be a candidate for a round or two in the ring. Yes, I was back to work. But I still had to fight the desire to withdraw from people and from life; I could barely concentrate; I had not one ounce of self-esteem left in my body; everything around me seemed gray and lifeless; and a tsunami of hopelessness washed over me about every five minutes.

Start with a heaping helping of Mary, throw in a few cupfuls of Martha, and almost anything is possible!

Thankfully, whenever I would start to zone out or get down on myself, my Mary-and-Martha team would snap into action. You can probably guess who said what:

"Here, wear this."

"Oh, yes! That will be perfect with your eyes."

"You're on in fifteen minutes. Now, wash your face."

"You know, I think you're just as pretty without makeup."

"Here's your microphone."

"Why don't you sing something funny to start?"

"I have the soundtrack ready."

"Okay, this is it."

"You can do this. I know you can."

Whenever I went to a new town or stepped onto a new stage, I just did what I knew to do, and the rest always seemed to follow. And when I didn't know, my traveling companions, Mary and Martha, were quick to tell me! They were a bright, flashing sign of God's loving kindness in the midst of my dark, gray world. I had no idea what I needed. I could not have planned such an itinerary. But the doctor (or was it the mortgage guy?) was right: I needed to go on with my life and my career. Thankfully, God was way ahead of me. He had already handpicked my Mary and Martha. He knew there would be times when I would need one or the other—and many times when I would need both.

CHONDA'S INBOX

To: Chonda
Subject: A light in the darkness
From: Paula

Dear Chonda,

Thank you for coming to our town. The evening was brilliant. Bravo! I am praying for your recovery, and I'm confident that you will learn in the dark what you never would have learned in the light. Dull lives make boring stories . . . not that you need more material! Thanks for everything. You are a light in the darkness.

Paula

expert
insight

Returning to the Battlefield

Sometimes the best way to handle depression while waiting for your medication to kick in is to get back to your routine. You may feel some trepidation, wondering, Am I ready to go back? What will my coworkers think if I return to work? What will the ladies say if I show up at the meeting? But the best way to get past that hurdle is to follow the Nike creed: Just do it. Don't allow paranoia to overcome you. Trust that the tasks you performed regularly before the onset of your illness are so ingrained that you'll surely succeed.

Routine is healing. It restores your self-esteem and gives you a sense of accomplishment and control—all very important to your recovery. Don't stay holed up in your house. Lean on a few trusted friends to help you get back to doing the things you used to do. Ask them to give you honest evaluations of how you're doing, and use their comments as checkpoints. If you have a formal job, talk to yourbossorsupervisorandbehonestaboutyoursymptoms and medications. Be adamant that you fully expect to recover, and believe it yourself. Then throw yourself into your work. Accomplishing even the smallest task will do wonders!

chapter

4

Like any other gift, the gift of grace
can be yours only if you reach out
and take it. Maybe being able to
reach out and take it is a gift too.

—Frederick Buechner

Fear not, for I have redeemed you;

I have summoned you by name;

you are mine.

When you pass through the waters,

I will be with you;

And when you pass through the rivers,

they will not sweep over you.

—Isaiah 43:1–2

i can see clearly now—not!

Emotion and chocolate are a lot alike: too much and you can get downright sick, too little and the world might as well end (that is, if you like chocolate as much as I do). We women are emotional creatures! Little girls may be made of "sugar and spice and everything nice"; but let enough time go by, and that recipe is sure to ferment into some sort of emotion.

How many of you have gone to see a chick flick—complete with someone giving flowers, someone getting flowers, dancing, romancing, a two-sided conversation—and then thought about walking into your house, slapping your husband, and saying, "Oh, why can't you be more romantic?" Surely I'm not the only one! Recently I watched a movie in which a husband secretly took dance lessons so he could surprise his wife by taking her dancing. I'm sorry, but stuff like that only happens in the movies—oh wait, that was a movie. See what I mean?

I saw another movie in which the husband and wife were both professional assassins (competing agents, at that), only neither one knew the secret identity of the other. Once they learned about each other's line of work, they went from having a fairly hum-drum marriage to trying to kill each other—with guns and knives and rocket launchers. I admit the scenario was a bit exaggerated. Still, as women, we can understand the range of emotion involved, can't we? If we allow our emotions to drive us in our homes and marriages, then someone could end up getting hurt—maybe even vaporized. Am I right?

> If we allow our emotions to drive us in our homes and marriages, then someone could end up getting hurt—maybe even vaporized.

Generally speaking, emotion is not a bad thing. We need it for expression. When little Tommy makes a goal in soccer, it's entirely appropriate to cheer like crazy. This lets little Tommy know how excited we are about his soccer skills (and informs the other parents that this is our child, and they had better not say anything bad about him or they risk sparking an entirely different emotion—but then, that would be a different chapter). And when Aunt Myrtle dies, it's right to weep, wail, and mourn to express our sense of grief and loss. In both situations, we feel somewhat purged for having gone to the emotional extreme. We have participated in the human experience.

But what if you whoop and holler and there's no soccer game? Or you cry and wail and Aunt Myrtle has only a head cold? What if you are _____ (fill in the blank with your favorite activity, such as shopping, water skiing, cooking, knitting, playing tennis, etc.) and suddenly—totally unannounced and unprovoked—you're hit with overwhelming feelings of depression that send you careening straight to the funeral end of the emotional scale?

In those cases, emotion is not your friend. It's out of synch with reality. That kind of emotion fuels depression—like gas on a fire. I've had to learn the hard way to keep the gas can far, far away, lest a spark become a bonfire (and not one of celebration either). I've also had to learn that it's okay to approach some things very unemotionally, very matter of fact—even God.

Caught Up in the Emotion

Not everything I learned growing up in church was healthy. I've joked for years that I got saved 342 times growing up. If it stormed or flashed lightning outside, I got saved. Or if there was a good-looking boy at the altar, I got saved! For the most part, my faith was framed by emotionally driven revival services—singin', shoutin', wavin' hankies, more singin', runnin' the aisles, Sister Sarah Simms wailin' and blubberin', and finally, more singin'. And then came the altar call. Whenever I went forward and stood up front near the preacher (most of the time, that was my dad), I got caught up in his bubble of praise, and I couldn't help but feel something. I couldn't help but cry. Couldn't help but sing. Couldn't help but praise. I believed all of that was real then. I still believe it was real.

The problem was, I came to believe more in the emotion of God than in the essence of God. I began to equate waves of emotion with the presence of God. The more emotional a service was, the more God was there. The less emotional . . . you can see where I'm going.

So imagine my distress when one day the tide of emotion pulled so far back that I found myself beached on dry, powdery sand. Dry and thirsty, I just wanted to feel again. I needed to feel God stirring in my soul. That was the only way I could be sure he was still there. So I listened to the best praise music I could find—and there's plenty out there. Do you know that seventeen different artists have recorded "Shout to the Lord"? And what a soul-stirring song that is! But not even "Shout to the Lord" could make me feel un-numb. I even found a Latino version—but I still couldn't muster so much as a clap or a toe tap.

In desperation I pulled out a ringer—one from the good ol' days of revival, one that's always a slam-dunk for bringin' 'em to the altar: "Amazing Grace." Four verses later—complete with key change and a choral crescendo midway through the fourth stanza—there was still nothing, not even a tear. It used to be that just thinking about either of these two songs would have taken me straight to the throne room of God himself. But those days seemed to be long gone.

There must be something wrong with me, I thought. Since I couldn't rejoice in the Lord, I figured I must have some hidden sin or spiritual deprivation in my life. Maybe if I could just remember what that hidden sin was, maybe if I could dig deep enough, I might find it. Then I could drag it out into the light of day, where it would shrivel up and blow away; and I could move on and sing praise music and once again feel God's presence. Until that happened, I was pretty sure God just didn't want to be around me—let alone live in my heart.

During one of my weekends at work after my big crash, Alison and I stood in the back of a huge arena. Twenty thousand women were singing.

With jubilant expressions and hands raised, most every woman around me was beaming and singing, "Our God is an awesome God." The entire room was glowing. This must be a small glimpse of heaven, I thought. Then Depression whispered, "I wonder if you'll ever be there. You certainly aren't feeling what these ladies are feeling."

"Okay, you know I don't do this —I'm Methodist. But I think God wants me to tell you something."

As a single, defeated tear rolled slowly down my cheek, Alison leaned over to me and said, "Okay, you know I don't do this—I'm Methodist. But I think God wants me to tell you something."

That certainly got my attention because . . . well, Alison is Methodist! I leaned my head down and moved my ear closer to her lips.

"God wants me to tell you, 'You're going to learn that your relationship with me is deeper than emotion, and understanding that will move you to a higher plane of worship.'"

I looked into Alison's eyes. Obviously she was as baffled as I was. She shrugged her shoulders. "Isn't that weird?" she said with an embarrassed grin. "I've never done that before." And we never spoke about it again.

Don't Cry for Me, Jamaica

Weeks later I found myself weeping on the most peaceful beach in Jamaica. (I know what you're thinking—what did I have to weep about? I was on a beach in Jamaica! Hang in there, I do have a point.) My husband was hoping that a little sunshine, the sound of waves breaking on the sand, and lots of island food would cheer me up. We'd actually had this vacation planned for some time. Alison and Ken came along with us. The men love to scuba dive, and Alison and I—well, we love to just sit in lounge chairs and do nothing. Alison is the greatest do-nothing-girlfriend in the world. We can do nothing together better than anyone else. In fact, some might say we are experts at doing nothing. Is there an award for that? If there is, I'm sure we're much too busy doing nothing to accept. But I digress . . .

I had been taking my medicine for about three or four weeks. I still had more bad days than good days, but the doctors had told me to expect that; most anti-depressants build up slowly in your system. On a good day I got my things packed for the trip, just in time for a bad day—when I cried at the airport. I pulled myself together and managed to get through customs. Then, a few hours later, while sitting on a tropical veranda with a Caribbean breeze blowing across my face, staring off into the most gorgeous blue water I'd ever seen, palm trees swaying gently, island music tinkling somewhere just behind a floral hedge, an exotic bird calling out something that sounded like "Welcome to paradise! Welcome to paradise!"—I wept.

Not even the delicious banana-flavored something I was drinking (non-alcoholic, of course! When you're depressed, it's important to limit your alcohol and caffeine intake to zero) could keep me from thinking, I shouldn't even be alive. I'm making the people I love miserable. I will never crawl out of this gray hole. My career is finished. My family will never look at me the same because of this pathetic life I'm living.

The warm tradewinds washed over me.

Nearby steel drums played something very Caribbean-like.

"Welcome to Paradise! Welcome to Paradise!"

And all I wanted to do—all I could do—was cry.

I apologized to a lot of people that weekend—to the umbrella man on the beach, to the waiter at the fancy restaurant, to the Russian couple who sat at our table at the all-you-can-eat beachside buffet. (They told us they were professionaldanceinstructors;sowhilethetikitorchesburned, Daviddemonstratedsomeofhisrobotdancemovesforthem.) Iespeciallykeptapologizingtomybestfriends,whoIbelieved desperately needed a vacation away from "people like me"!

But my best friends also have pretty cool day jobs (no, they're not professional dance instructors). As I already mentioned, Alison is a full-time licensed counselor and Ken is a doctor, a general practitioner. They are both gifts to their communities and to the people of South Carolina—and particularly to those who struggle with mental illness. They treattheillnesswithmedicationandthementalwithloveand prayer.Icouldn'thavehandpickedtwobetter-qualifiedpeople to be stranded with me on my own personal deserted island.

One evening at sunset, I had a breakthrough. I sat quietly and watched the sun—a beautiful ball of orange fire—drop slowly into the ocean. Through tear-blurred vision, I saw it disappear peacefully into the blue. And as objectively as possible, I thought, That was beautiful. There was no song or swellofemotionthatbroughtmetothatconclusion.Thesight ofafiery-orangesundisappearingintoanendlessexpanseof blueseaisathingofbeauty—alwayshasbeen,alwayswillbe. Some things can't be denied, no matter how you feel.

At that moment I realized that the presence of God is

like the splendor of the sunset: It can't be denied, no matter how you feel. God manifests his presence in many ways that are not emotionally driven—in warm winds, the smell of sea salt, the trilling of birds, the setting of the sun. His signature is at the bottom of every great work of art and under the title of every beautiful song. I don't have to feel as if I just left a romantic chic-flick to know that my husband loves me. And I don't have to feel the euphoria of a heart-pounding, hanky-waving revival sermon to know that I've been saved.

Depression taught me a great lesson that weekend: Feelings are temporary. Sometimes they even lie. From that evening forward, I began to lean more on what I know and less on what I feel.

I know God is a big God.

I know God wants the best for me.

I know God holds my future in his hands.

I know God is in control.

I know God loves me.

I know God is an awesome God.

I'd like to say that I came all the way around that weekend. That Alison, Ken, David, and I laughed and ate tons of island food and danced with the Russians. But the fact is, I cried a lot, and I didn't eat much. And most of the beauty I saw was blurred behind tears.

But what I did do was to be still and know that he is God, as Psalm 46:10 says. I invested in that verse totally. I even sunburned on one side, I was so still. In the process, I realized there was nothing wrong between God and me. No deep, dark, secret sin, as I had feared. I didn't have to feel God to know he was right there beside me—even living within me.

Seems I found God in a very matter-of-fact way in Jamaica. God abides in and out of emotion—whether we're singing "Shout to the Lord" (Spanish or English version) or simply feeling numb. God is God. God is.

On the plane ride home, I remembered something—or at least I thought I remembered it. I had been in a fog of depression, so I couldn't be sure. So I asked David: "Did you really do the robot dance for those professional dance instructors from Russia?"

David turned and—as much as the tray table in front of him would allow—brought his right arm up, lever-like, then smacked his right hand down with his left one so that his right arm seemed to drop suddenly, pendulum-like. Just like a robotic arm.

"They were very complimentary," he said in all seriousness.

That made me smile.

✉ CHONDA'S INBOX

To: Chonda
Subject: Hope to women
From: Karen

Dear Chonda,

I recently had the opportunity to hear part of your personal testimony and was amazed at how much my life has mirrored yours. I am dealing with a lot of emotional issues that seem overwhelming at times. Your testimony reminds me of God's faithfulness and his ability to heal all wounds. You are a great encouragement, and I appreciate your willingness to share from your life experiences. You give hope to women like me.

Karen

expert
insight

Don't Go by Feelings

Depressed people frequently make poor choices when they "just don't feel right." Sometimes, in an effort to feel better, they turn to alcohol or drugs. This is called "self-medicating," and it's often the start of a horrible habit—one that not only interferes with their antidepressant medications but also creates a whole new set of potentially lifelong problems.

Don't go there! And don't try to measure your progress based on how you feel. You're not in a good mental state to do so! A depressed person is already pessimistic and has a negative opinion of herself. When you judge yourself according to your feelings, you automatically start from a point of disadvantage.

chapter 4

Instead of asking yourself if you're "feeling better," try a different yardstick: Am I crying less? Am I sleeping better? Do I like myself more? Am I more hopeful? Answering these questions honestly will help you measure your progress much more accurately than going by your feelings. Consider enlisting a trusted friend to help you ask the right questions and give objective answers.

chapter
5

Why is it that when we talk to God, we are
said to be praying, and when God
talks to us, we are said to be schizophrenic?

—Lily Tomlin

Anxiety in a man's heart weighs it down,

but a good word makes it glad.

—Proverbs 12:25 NASB

friends don't let friends talk to themselves

The first time I sat in a counselor's office, I was nineteen years old. It was a small office above a clothing store in a small town in Tennessee. I went because my mother asked me to go. Some mothers believe their daughters need to trim their bangs, lengthen their skirts, or not use so much lipstick. Mine believed I needed counseling.

I guess I can understand why. Over a two-year period, when I was in my mid-teens, my two sisters passed away. Charlotta, at twenty years old, died in a car accident. About twenty months later, Cheralyn, the baby of the family, came down with what we thought was the flu—but turned out to be a powerful form of leukemia. She died twenty-one days after her diagnosis. Between their deaths my father packed up and left. He chose to leave on my brother's wedding day. While the house buzzed with wedding preparations, my father packed his bags; and after he pronounced Mike and Doris man and wife—while the house was filled with the happy sound of wrapping paper being ripped from wedding gifts—he left.

I was eighteen by the time the dust settled, and a year into our "grief recovery period." At an age when other girls were filled with excitement and expectation, I was empty—empty of hopes, dreams, even tears. My tear ducts had simply dried up. Is that possible?

> My tear ducts had simply dried up. Is that possible?

Looking back, I believe I built a wall in my heart bigger than the Hoover Dam. Only instead of concrete, I used something like those sandbags you see people on the Weather Channel stacking up at the edge of a rising river, trying to keep dangerous waters from flooding the banks and washing away their homes. I was trying to hold back the tears and, with them, the emotions that I was afraid would overwhelm my life. Instead of sand, I filled my bags with bitterness and sarcasm. Those are two things that can stop a torrent of tears—for a while anyway. I became the queen of sarcasm.

"Go to your room!" my mother would tell me, fed up and put out with my sarcasm. Of course, we would both be standing in the bedroom of our one-bedroom apartment. "This is my room!" I would fire back.

And so my mother suggested that we take a trip together to the counselor's office.

I remember that meeting. Boy, did the sandbags hold. Nothing leaked through. But I was honest.

"How do you feel about your sisters dying?"

"Angry."

"How do you feel about your father leaving?"

"Angry."

"How do you feel about God?"

"Angry."

There was no big break-through moment. No group hug. I didn't even get a pat on the back. But sitting down and talking things out did seem to take the edge off a bit; and overall, I thought I handled my trip to the counselor pretty well. Mom even let me come out of my room.

After that, life took over and I got busy. I figured either (1) I was healed, or (2) the dam was holding. Either way, I could function, and that was the important thing. You just can't beat practical, basic functionality. Until you come face to face with the divine.

Divine Conversations

Have you ever had someone give you "a word from the Lord"? About twenty years ago, far away from home, I got one of them; and every time I think about it, I still get cold chills. I'm not a theologian, and I can't explain all the spiritual ins and outs of prophecy to you. (And please don't ask Alison to explain; she's Methodist.) I just know that a complete stranger came up to me in a church in California and said, "Take your hands off and let me do the work. I will put your name in lights, and you will glorify your Father." And then he walked away.

I wasn't in California to entertain anyone. I was passing through, and I had slipped into a church service. No one there knew my name, much less what I dreamed of doing for a living. I didn't even know what I wanted to do back then! But when that stranger spoke that word to me, I felt the shiver of God's presence and truth for days.

About ten years later, in November 1996, David and I were sitting in the office of Dr. David Gatewood at the headquarters of Focus on the Family in Colorado Springs.

We had traveled to Colorado to visit the Focus facility and talk with someone about a ministry we were trying to get off the ground to help preacher's kids. Dr. Gatewood was a preacher's kid; he was also the head of the Focus on the Family counseling department and a very tender, soft-spoken man. His wife joined us, and the four of us ended our visit with a word of prayer.

But somewhere between Dr. Gatewood's "Dear heavenly Father, we come before you . . ." and ". . . amen," something happened. There was a long, almost uncomfortable pause. I squeezed my husband's hand and was about to take a peek to see if Dr. Gatewood was still in the room, when he began praying again. This time, though, the phrasing was different. His voice inflection changed. The quiet, tender man we'd visited with all day long began to speak powerfully and directly about things he could not have possibly known about us—personal things.

I peeked and saw his wife reach for a notepad and pencil. She began to write down everything her husband said (so that we wouldn't forget, she told us later). I got that same presence-of-God shiver I'd felt years earlier in California.

Dr. Gatewood passed away several years after our meeting. But even now I occasionally take out that crumpled piece of paper from my jewelry box, read the transcript of our divine conversation with heaven, and weep. I won't share the entire message with you. Frankly, most if it is none of your business! And some parts of it I still don't completely understand. But most if it—almost all of it—has incredible relevance even now:

"My special rhinestone cowgirl, have I not given you the spirit of clowning? But my clowns are filled with tears. Your laughter without tears would not be laughter at all, my zealous, zestful daughter! I have called you to minister to my people out of the tragedies of your life. I will put your name in lights more than you know. But let me do the work. I will do it. . . .

"Have I not called you to joy and peace and serenity? With me, there is no striving. Hear this, my daughter, I have striven for you already. Your call is to walk in the wake of my striving. These are the mysteries of my Spirit. Ponder them and I will show you the way. . . .

"I would hug you my daughter. Come to me for your daily hug! I am not like your father. I am meek and humble in spirit, and you will have rest for your soul. Teach my people wide-eyed wonder! Little-girl sparkles! Childlike laughter! I have not left you alone. . . . Your sensitive lover,

David, was prepared before you were born. Silent lips, deep waters—have you not given him your doleful tears? Has he not been your stately stag?

"This is my promise: . . . come to my rock, sit under my shelter, bask in my warmth, even as David did in Psalms 61 and 62. . . . Enough of the terrors of the night. Enough of the flying darts of the evil one. Enough of the fowler's snare. . .

"My special rhinestone cowgirl, have I not given you the spirit of clowning?"

. Bright lights! Bright spotlights! You will see your name in greater lights, if you honor me. I will honor you before a broken and hurt generation. Remember this is my work, my daughter."

Oh my! Have I spooked you yet? Can you stand one more?

Just a few years ago, my phone rang, and I heard the voice of my colleague Dan Rupple on the line. We exchanged the normal pleasantries.

"How are the kids?"

"Fine. Yours?"

"Fine. How's work?"

"Good."

Dan is one of the founding members of the Isaac Airfreight comedy troupe. When I was a kid, I used to lie on the floor in the living room and roll with laughter as I listened to the group's antics on one of their first LPs! It amazes me that our paths eventually crossed, and Dan and I are now good friends and partners. We even started an organization together called the Christian Comedy Association, which has grown to over 250 members—comics, ventriloquists, writers, TV personalities, and other folks interested in comedy and Christ.

Anyway, back to the phone call. I'll never forget Dan, who was a pastor at the time, trying so hard to preface what he was about to say, as if I might think he was crazy. (I already think he's crazy; he could never mess that up!) Haltingly, he began telling me about a sweet prayer warrior who prays for his family regularly—a wonderful prayer partner who is a real strength to his ministry—even though she happens to live in Italy—and occasionally she speaks into their lives in a prophetic way and . . .

"Dan, that's wonderful," I interrupted. "Don't worry, I get it. I don't understand it, but I get it. What's up?"

"Chonda," he said, "this lady doesn't know anything about our work in Christian comedy. She is not familiar with you or your career. But she told me of a dream she had, and she described you to a T. I know beyond a shadow of a doubt that she was talking about you."

As Dan went on to share this woman's vision, I sat speechless at my desk. Then suddenly my mind raced back to Dr. Gatewood's office. I grabbed a pad and pencil and began writing down every word I could catch.

"This woman had a dream three nights in a row," Dan said. "You, a high-profile football player, and another person were standing on top of a snow-covered mountain. God's hand reached down and, one by one, gently pushed each of you off. The third person stopped dead in his tracks. The football player rolled a bit but eventually got stuck almost comically in a snowball, with his skis buried in the landscape. You—you tumbled and rolled for a long distance until you were out of sight. As you rolled you became a giant snowball, round but not filled with snow—filled with blessings. And then she woke up."

Dan told me as much as he could remember about the dream, and then he hung up the phone. Was this another divine conversation? Was the woman's dream a prophetic "heads-up" about my upcoming roll towards the depths of depression? Was it a word of encouragement to let me know that my fall would ultimately bring blessing to others?

And, by the way, what was up with the football player?

You tell me.

One Sandbag at a Time

I believe that divine conversations happen. God loves to work in surprising and miraculous ways. Sometimes divine conversations are of the more ordinary kind, however. They take place between you and a friend or you and a counselor. These conversations, too, can give you the God-is-in-the-house shivers.

I also believe that divine healing happens—although sometimes it takes more than a few divine appointments (whether prophetic or ordinary) to see a healing all the way through. It's like penicillin; penicillin is a great healing agent, but most of the time you have to take more than a few doses if you want to get rid of your infection.

I have never heard of anyone walking into a counselor's office for the first time, sitting down, having a conversation, and then walking out healed and whole. No, for counseling to be effective, you have to make a commitment to spend whatever time it takes to unravel the mystery, to peel away a few layers—or in my case, to open the floodgates. My one little visit at the age of nineteen definitely didn't do it.

After my big crash, I talked to my psychologist-friend Alison a lot. She and my sister-in-law, Doris, helped me through my first few times back on stage. Somehow I survived. But when it was time for me to head back to work on a regular basis, I was terrified. I knew I was booked to stay in nice hotels, but in my mind I was still holed up at the gray hotel, with the talking lights. What if I had a meltdown in front of an audience? People buy tickets to come laugh with me. I was pretty sure they wouldn't be interested in a comedian who just stood there and cried all night!

So Alison climbed on the bus and helped me finish up the tour I had started with singer Sandi Patty. "The Girls Are Back in Town Tour" was a hit, and so was my new friendship with Sandi. Sandi is a seasoned professional who has performed with symphonies and before sitting presidents and other dignitaries. She is also a seasoned Christian woman who has seen dark days, as well as glorious ones. She knows what it feels like to keep going when you feel as if the world is caving in on you. Looking back, I can see that touring with

> I was pretty sure they wouldn't be interested in a comedian who just stood there and cried all night!

Sandi was, in its own way, a divine appointment that only God could have orchestrated at that time in my life.

After "The Girls Are Back in Town," I was contracted to speak at more than twenty-five pre-conference sessions for Women of Faith. To be fair to the organization (and to the thousands of women who would be attending their conferences), I told Mary Graham, president of Women of Faith, that I had been diagnosed with clinical depression.

"If you want to get someone else, I understand," I told her.

Mary didn't flinch. She just put her arm around me and said, "Chonda, you do what you do, and God will do the rest." (Another divine appointment!) "Besides," she continued, "this is a pretty safe place to fall apart. You are among people who adore you."

So I asked Alison the one question I had never asked her in our thirty-five years of friendship: "How much do you get paid?" I couldn't expect her to travel along with me to the conferences and miss so much of her own work without getting compensated! I was already depressed—destroying my best friend's livelihood would only have made me feel worse.

We came up with a plan: Matt, my road manager, would take care of the traveling logistics, and I would pay Alison counseling fees for the three days she would be with me each weekend. That way, when I found myself curled up in the bed in some gray hotel room sobbing into a pillow, she could ask me her "shrink questions," and I wouldn't feel guilty keeping her awake half the night. (I'm sure if she knew then what she knows now, she would have asked for more money!)

My work visits with Alison were divine appointments— I'm sure of it. Each weekend we would tear open another sandbag, and each weekend more water would woosh out of me. Afterward Alison would go back to South Carolina, and I would go back to Tennessee. Unfortunately, this didn't make for an easy week for either of us. Let me put it this way: Long-distance counseling is never a good idea. The problem isn't the high phone bills or the tired fingers from typing all those e-mails. The problem is that the counselor can't see the whites of her client's eyes. And the client can't see just how quickly the counselor would like to smack her with a baseball bat. (Wait—maybe long-distance counseling is a good idea. At least it's safe!)

Understand, I love professionals. I find it hard to contradict all their years of learning and training. I'm awed by all the degrees after their names and all the diplomas on their walls. But when the professional is your best friend...? When you've seen her fat and pregnant, poor and miserable, broken and terrified . . . ? (Yep, we've been through all that and more). Then you have a tendency to discount her advice, or worse: just plain refuse to do it. I remember telling Alison at one point, "Why can't you just be my friend and quit telling me what to do all the time?" I hear my voice speaking those words today, and my face is flush with shame!

I'm grateful that Alison is a professional. At least she knows when a client is responding to trauma, reacting to a new medicine, or just being downright ornery.

After a while we both knew it was time for me to find a counselor who was not too attached—someone I was not so familiar with. Alison's husband, Ken, said it best: "Our friendship is the most important thing. Someone else can treat you; we want to be your friends for life."

So I stepped into my new counselor's office. She had a nice, big, cushy sofa—and no baseball bat in the corner. She sat across from me, studying my sandbags, asking me questions. Close by sat a box of tissues, in case the dam should break.

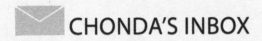# CHONDA'S INBOX

To: Chonda
Subject: Thank you for the laughter
From: Kim

Hello Chonda,

It's amazing how God works through others! I am not sure how to say what I am thinking except to offer a big thank you. I was one of those people who didn't think that depression was real until I went through it myself. I believe that if Christians could learn what depression is really about, they would not look at it as if it were leprosy, and those who go through depression would look for help and healing before it's too late.

Thank you for laughter. It is definitely what the doctor ordered.

Kim

expert
insight

Finding the Best Counselor

Getting an accurate diagnosis and starting on the right medication, if recommended, are two of the most important tools in curing depression. Finding a professional counselor who best fits your needs is another. It's imperative that you find a counselor you trust and who makes you feel comfortable. Not only must you feel you can depend on this person's confidentiality, but you must trust his or her professional ability—otherwise you will never pour out your deepest pain or darkest secrets.

Counselors come in many shapes and sizes and with varying credentials. Clinical social workers, mental health counselors, psychologists, and psychiatrists have received specific training (at various levels) and have been licensed to deal with depression and other mental health issues. Often it is possible to find a licensed counselor or psychotherapist who shares your Christian faith—a factor that can make a significant difference in his or her approach to the issues in your life. Good Web sites for finding qualified Christian counselors are www.aacc.net or www.findchristiancounselors.com.

Churches are often the best source for recommendations of licensed Christian counselors who are practicing in a particular area. Some churches even have licensed counselors on staff. And if they don't, they usually offer pastoral or lay counseling programs, although the individuals involved typically don't have the training or credentials to make a diagnosis of clinical depression. Prayer and lay counseling are helpful in many situations; but if you suspect that you are depressed, don't hesitate to ask for and seek out professional help.

chapter
6

If you can't get rid of the skeleton in your
closet, you'd best teach it to dance.

—George Bernard Shaw

Form your purpose by asking for

counsel, then carry it out

using all the help you can get.

Proverbs 20:18 MSG

what do you think she's going to say?

We have a little phrase around my house that we use whenever we find ourselves in the middle of world that is new to us, surrounded by people we don't know, wondering what their response to us might be: "What do you think they're going to say?"

Most of the time that phrase is tinged with excitement—when we're waiting for an important phone call, for example. Early in my career, I would have meetings with entertainment executives who were in a position to help me succeed. They would listen to me tell jokes, and then I would go home and wait to hear back from them. Did they like me? Did they think I was funny? All night long I would toss and turn, and every five minutes I'd ask David, "What do you think they're going to say?"

For the first twelve years of our marriage, David worked tough maintenance jobs. He spent long, grueling hours on roof tops in the worst of weather—snow, ice, and freezing temperatures in the winter, scorching heat in the summer.

So when I would ask him in the middle of the night, "What do you think they're going to say?" he'd usually answer with something like, "That your husband can retire and fish all day!"

> Back then we seemed to hold our breath a lot. We put a lot of weight on what people we didn't know might say.

Back then we seemed to hold our breath a lot. We put a lot of weight on what people we didn't know might say. Now we poke fun at ourselves by using the phrase all the time. Sitting at the dentist's office waiting for Zach's wisdom teeth to be pulled, I asked, "What do you think they're going to say, Zach?" He rolled his eyes and responded, "That I need to eat more candy!"

David eventually left the maintenance business. To this day he shivers at the sight of an air-conditioning unit, whether it's running or not. He went back to school, earned his masters degree in English, and went on to teach composition at Middle Tennessee University. His classes gained a great reputation—so much so that students dropped other classes just to sit in on one of his writing classes. (Obviously I am prejudiced, proud, and smitten by my professor!) In his spare time, David wrote and sent out manuscripts and made contacts with literary agents. When the publishing floodgates started opening and his phone began to ring, the kids and I would laugh out loud every time he would ask, "What do you think they're going to say?"

"He's getting you back, Mom!" Chera would holler.

Where Are the Doughnuts?

It's funny how much importance we place on what others might say about the way we act, work, play, sing, tell jokes, write, or whatever. Will the Grand Ole Opry call after they've looked at your press kit? Are you funny enough for prime time TV? Will the publisher accept your manuscript—maybe even give you an advance? "What do you think they're going to say?" becomes loaded with possibilities—exciting, hold-your-breath possibilities.

But then there are the possibilities that are not so exciting. They're downright scary.

I remember my first meeting with another professional

who knew her business well. She sat and listened to me carefully, scribbling notes and peering over the top of her glasses. Our appointment was for an hour, but not too long into our meeting I wondered if an hour, was going to be enough to even get started—and whether this woman had enough paper to write on. The thought, What do you think she's going to say? was neither funny nor exciting. It was terrifying.

David drove me to that first meeting at my new counselor's office. She is a soft-spoken, brilliant woman. I had talked to her a couple of times on the phone, and she came highly recommended by several friends. I asked Alison to pass along my chart. I knew I could trust Alison's notes.

She worked from her house in a quiet suburb, so there's no big parking lot to pull into while you wait for your turn to go in. You have to park on the street and watch for the person with the appointment ahead of you to leave. So there we were, David and I, sitting in the car in a shady spot on the shoulder of the road, waiting for her current client to come out of the house and move his or her car. As other cars passed by slowly, I shielded my face or pretended to be busy with the radio. It felt like a police stakeout, minus the doughnuts and coffee.

Before long our "suspect" exited the building—male, five-foot-eleven, heavy-set, salt-and-pepper hair. I wondered what he was in for. Why was he seeing a therapist? To look at him, you never would have guessed that he had just spent an hour spilling his guts to a complete stranger. Suspiciously, he got into his car, turned the ignition, and slowly backed out of the driveway. Well, actually, there was nothing suspicious about him; the whole scene just felt suspicious. As he pulled away, he glanced towards me. I started punching the presets on the radio so I wouldn't have to make eye contact.

"Wonder why he's here?" David asked.

I looked at my husband and thought, I love this man! Apparently I wasn't the only one playing detective.

Balancing the Baggage

Why does going to see a psychologist, a counselor, or a psychiatrist have such a stigma attached to it? Maybe in L.A. it's a cool thing to have your therapist on speed dial. But in the South, we're supposed to have family—moms and dads and grandparents and aunts and uncles and a zillion cousins—to fall back on when times are tough. Not to mention, we have a church (sometimes two) on every corner. Here in the South, we shouldn't have to go to complete strangers and pay them to listen to us talk about our troubles. What would people say?

That's exactly what I was wondering as I stepped onto the sun porch of the office. All my baggage about seeking psychological help was balanced precariously on my shoulders as I rang the doorbell. In my case, I couldn't fall back on my family—at least not certain branches of it. They were not part of the solution. They were part of the problem.

You see, I have a troublesome gene in my physical makeup. My father was manic-depressive most of my childhood. "Bipolar" is the clinical term, and I have always been terrified of the possibility that that particular chromosome might show up somewhere in my body. For years I watched his mood swings wreak havoc on our lives. He capped off most every "high" with a move into a new house or the purchase of a new car or something else expensive that sent us into debt. Or worse, he turned to infidelity. My parents' marriage never was the biblical love nest I heard him preach about on Sunday mornings.

The "lows" were terrifying. I can't count the number of nights my father came into my bedroom, as if to tuck me in, toting a loaded gun—one of those small handguns that was steely and dark in his grip, heavy enough to mash what do you think she's going to say?

the soft blankets when he put it down just long enough to kiss me good-night (good-bye?) and weep over me. I suppose he thought he was being helpful when he rattled off thorough instructions on what to do with his body and how to clean the blood stains from the carpet.

My brother, Mike, and I have a lot of the same genes. (Have you seen our noses? I rest my case.) But as with all forms of divvying-up, someone always get more of one thing than another. Mike tells me that I have the "run your mouth" gene. He's probably right about

> I can't count the number of nights my father came into my bedroom, as if to tuck me in, toting a loaded gun.

that. I do tend to gush. But I'm convinced my job as a comedian has been a healthy outlet for me to learn how not to keep too much locked in. Learning what is appropriate to spill out . . . well, that's something I'm still working on.

Mike, on the other hand, took his own scars from our childhood and buried them deep within. He rarely talked about our past, and when I was asked to write a book about it, he objected.

"Why would you want to do that? Who would believe

it? And why would anyone ever want to read that mess? It's an embarrassment. Besides, you never know what Dad will do if you start putting the truth out there." (When I told this to my new counselor, she scribbled like crazy on her yellow pad.)

Finally we came to a peaceful arrangement: Mike would never read anything I wrote or watch anything I recorded. That worked for me, but eventually it stopped working for him. (You can find out why by reading his story—it's a doozy!—in his own words. It's on his Web site, www.mikeanddoris.com.)

As I waited on my counselor's porch, I began to wonder if she would be able to spot a rogue gene in me. Surely, if she was any good at all, she would catch it in the tone of my "hello." I stood at the door, the muted dong of the bell dying away, and looked back at David. He was in the car, messing with the radio. When he looked up, I recognized his expression instantly. I'm sure he recognized mine too: What do you think she's going to say?

Old Ghosts and Demons

Whenever I have written or spoken about my life story, I have always tried to honor my parents as much as possible. Years ago I reached a point of peace with my dad. Through a wonderful prayer session with Lana Bateman, an author and prayer minister who travels with Women of Faith as a chaplain for the speakers, I learned how to see God as my loving heavenly Father—and how to look at my broken earthly father with tender compassion. Basically, my father is an intelligent man, energetic and likeable. There is nothing he cannot build or fix, and no one would leave his presence thinking he was a menace to society. Yet he is broken. And either the discipline to take the necessary medication for bipolar disorder never found its way into his life, or someone, somewhere, convinced him he didn't need the help.

He divorced my mom when I was eighteen, and he remarried—twice. At the time of this writing, at least a dozen years have passed since I last talked to him. However, our lives rammed smack into each other just a few years back. It was an experience that was both numbing and sickening for me. I'm sure it was no picnic for him either.

I got a call out of the clear blue from a young woman who claimed to be "my sister." I had to stop and think for a moment. Both my sisters were in heaven. I pinched myself—yep, I was wide awake. And then I remembered that my father had adopted his new wife's children. She had several boys and a daughter. That daughter was the woman on the other line. I'll call her "Susan."

Susan explained that she had read a couple of my books and watched a few of my comedy videos lately. The books and videos were never allowed in her house when she was a kid; but now that she was out and on her own, curiosity got the best of her.

> "Do you know how nervous you make Dad? I think it's because you've always spoken up and told the truth!"

Then she said something that made my stomach turn. She was going to trial soon. Would it be okay if she gave my name and phone number to the attorney prosecuting her case? I wanted to throw up. She didn't have to say another word; I knew what the trial was about.

I told her I had not seen my father in several years. He had come with his family to one of my nephew's graduations, but he didn't have much to say to me or my kids. He spent most of the picnic hunkered down at a table with his wife and children, and when I walked over to say hello, he only nodded. No one spoke.

Susan chuckled and said she remembered that incident.

"Do you know how nervous you make Dad? I think it's because you've always spoken up and told the truth!" Then we laughed like two kids staying up late after curfew—like sisters.

"If there is anything I can do, I will," I told her.

"Maybe there is," she said. She explained that she had been "reading between the lines" of one of my books and wondered if we had been through the same abuse. Maybe we had similar stories. I stopped her in midsentence.

"Let's not swap war stories," I said. "Let's leave them for your attorney." I'm sure part of my hesitancy was simple self-preservation. I didn't want to drudge up old memories. And part of it was a God-thing. "Let's not give Dad any reason to think that we got our stories together, and we're ganging up on him. Just have the district attorney call me, and I will tell him what I remember about my childhood."

After we hung up, I sat and stared at the walls in my office for what seemed like hours. Eventually David walked in.

"You look like you've seen a ghost," he said.

"More like an old demon," I answered, and I told him about the phone call.

"So the DA's office will be calling you?"

113

I nodded and bit my lip to keep from crying. "What do you think he's going to say?"

The next morning the phone rang, and the caller identified himself as the prosecuting attorney for a particular county in a nearby state. (I'm being deliberately vague here.) He told me he was prosecuting my father on several counts of child molestation and endangerment, and he asked if I had any information that might strengthen his case.

I found a comfortable spot on the floor and sat there, leaning my back against the wall. I was determined to be as open as possible about my past, while still maintaining some sense of compassion for my parents. I didn't want to seem accusatory, and I definitely didn't want to be viewed as a victim. God had delivered me from a mound of dysfunction, so why give Satan an ounce of credit by rehashing or romanticizing the details?

Unfortunately, until that moment, I had convinced myself that the abuse I suffered had been a one-time thing—that the circumstances surrounding those days of my childhood were so unique that none of what happened could possibly repeat itself. But now, hearing an "official" voice—one belonging to a man who handed out one-way tickets to jail, when he did his job right—triggered a remarkable amount of guilt in my heart: not for what I'd done, but for what I hadn't done.

"I'm so sorry I wasn't as brave as this young woman," I told the attorney through sobs. "Maybe if I'd said something earlier, it might have saved her from all this."

"Well, it just might have," he said with a dispassionate tone.

He told me where and when I needed to show up at his office to give an official deposition. I jotted down the details, and we hung up. But before I put the phone back in its cradle, I dialed Alison's number. "You're not going to believe what has happened . . ."

The next day David and I drove several hours to the courthouse. I spent most of the time on the cell phone with my pastor and with Alison, praying and counseling. I was afraid of opening old wounds and revealing too much of myself in my semi-public life. Worse, I was terrified of what people might say.

We finally arrived, parked the car, and walked into the courthouse, where someone steered us to a conference room filled with a long oak table and several chairs. Everything smelled like furniture polish. A man walked in and introduced himself, and I quickly recognized his gritty voice from our phone conversation. He slapped a yellow legal pad on the table and told me that he simply needed to establish the fact that what had happened to me was similar to what had happened to his client.

I explained that I didn't know the details of Susan's allegations—that I had stopped her from telling them to me so that no one could say we got our stories together.

"What in the world prompted you to do that?" the attorney said. "That's brilliant!"

"Well, I know my dad, and he's pretty convincing," I answered. "He will make you believe that we are all crazy and that he is one of the godliest men in the universe. I think he's a very sick man."

The attorney's eyes narrowed. "I don't think he's sick," he said coolly. "I think he's downright evil, and I plan to see him pay for all of this."

Suddenly I had a strange, disquieting feeling: I was afraid for my father.

For the next couple of hours, the district attorney asked me questions—most of them extremely personal. He wrote things down, stopped and thought to himself, then asked more questions, steering me toward specific details. Finally he stood up.

"I think that's all I need for now," he said. "We may or may not be able to use this information. But I'll be curious what do you think she's going to say?

to see what your father's reaction is when I place your name on the witness list."

Maybe he was curious, but I wasn't.

David and I left the courthouse, and just as we were climbing into our car, another car pulled into the parking lot. What if that's my dad's car? I thought, and my heart began to pound. But then a woman with graying hair climbed out of the driver's side, spotted me, and called out, "Chonda, is that you?"

I was so glad to see that the driver was not my dad, but my father's second wife—not the third wife with the children, but the wife he'd left my mother for. The district attorney had called her in for questioning too. I'd heard about her divorce from my dad. Apparently, she was more of a fighter than my mother. She even took the seats off the toilet when she left!

We hugged and swapped pleasantries. She hadn't seen my kids for at least ten years, so I showed her pictures. Any resentment or ill feelings from the past seemed to melt away. Maybe it was because we had a common link, a common story, a common cause: We both had survived the same storm.

> Ill feelings from the past seemed to melt away. We both had survived the same storm.

On the long drive home, David and I discussed all the possible legal scenarios of the case—like we really knew what they were. We'd only learned the word deposition that week. Several days went by with no word from the DA's office. We passed the time by taking turns asking, "What do you think he's going to say?"

Finally the attorney called. He said he had decided that my testimony about my father was too old. It would be too easy for the defense to have it thrown out or dismissed. "But would you be willing to come to the trial anyway?" he asked. He explained that my presence would be "unwanted" there, and he could use that discomfort to his advantage.

"I want you to wait in a room in the courthouse. When I put your dad on the stand, you walk in and sit right behind me. I don't know if you know this, but your dad pretty much hates you. I'm hoping your presence will trip him up, and the judge will see what he's really made of."

It sounded like an old Perry Mason episode to me, but I agreed.

The night before the trial, David and I checked into a hotel room near the courthouse. But we never made it into court. In the morning the district attorney called and said, "Don't waste a trip. Your dad just walked into the courtroom and pled guilty. It's over."

And I was relieved. Truly relieved.

Pages from the Past

This is the story I had gathered together and put into a fresh file in the front of my mind, ready to pull out during my first visit with my counselor. What a great story to start a therapy session with, I figured. But halfway through our "get to know you" time, she threw me a curve ball. "Could you tell me a little bit about your childhood?" she asked.

Oh boy—that was a much larger file! I took a deep breath and poured out the pages:

"I lost my sisters when I was in high school. They died. One was twenty, the other was fifteen. I know that led me to have trust issues. I had a hard time allowing myself to have close friendships; but somehow I got past that, and I have managed to accumulate some very deep and meaningful relationships with several girlfriends who are very much like sisters to me."

Breathe.

"My father was emotionally and physically abusive. He was a pastor. I know that led me to have a distorted view of God as my Father. I never trusted clergy much

119

after that; but somehow I have developed a very strong, respectful relationship with my pastor. I went through a time of deliverance prayer, Bible study, and counseling that led to several breakthrough moments. Now I can honestly say I love my dad, although I am very sad for his life. I have experienced a true release from responsibility. I know I can't fix my dad, and it's not healthy for me to be engaged in a relationship with him—that would be toxic and dangerous. For me, peace is in letting him go."

Breathe.

"I have a brother; he is seven years older than me. As the firstborn in our family, he is the one who had to step up and fill in the dad-gap when we were growing up. But he's a mess right now, and most days I either want to cry for him or slap him. I just look at his life and think, That could be me.

Breathe.

"And then there's my mother. She's a funny one! Like, just the other day, she told me she is blessed because she knows that she has two daughters in heaven with Jesus right now, and God has allowed her to live this long because she still has two more kids to go. I thought, I'm forty-five years old, I've done my very best to serve God and live a holy life, and my mom still isn't sure I'm going to heaven! But instead of arguing about it, I just laughed. That's progress, believe me. Actually, my relationship with my mom is good. But we have battled over everything from religious legalism to letting me be an adult woman. She doesn't like my opinion on either subject, frankly! Of course, giving her the book Boundaries was not a good choice for a Mother's Day present a few years ago. But I know my mother has been through a great deal. She may not have handled everything correctly. Still, I'm thoroughly convinced that she loves me and that she didn't have a clue how much harm she was doing in the long run. We have resolved many issues; and I think the success of my career, in spite of my childhood, has been a huge teaching tool for Mom. She has learned that the truth can set you free . . ."

I was interrupted by a raised hand, her other one scrawling madly on the pad. I took a deep breath. When she stopped scribbling, she flexed her writing fingers and said, "Sounds like you've done a lot of work on this already."

I shrugged. "I thought I had. But now all of a sudden I'm deeply depressed, dead tired, and God has flown the coop. I feel totally alone and abandoned, everything around me seems dull and gray, and I'm terrified for the phone to ring. Every time it does, I wonder, What more does this world want to drain from me? I know that something is very wrong."

That's when I began to cry. I just blubbered all over myself. My compassionate counselor handed me the whole box of tissues. Then she studied her schedule book, and I thought, Oh boy, she's going to have to clear the next six months to figure this one out.

She closed her notepad. I stopped sniveling and said, "Okay, Doc. Give it to me straight. How bad is it?"

Softly she said, "Frankly, I see one tired, worn-out gal in front of me."

Before I could respond, she added, "I want to give you an assignment."

I pulled my shoulders up. I should have known there would be heavy lifting involved—more smothering layers to peel away, piece by painful piece. I dug my Palm Pilot from my purse and sat with my fingers poised over the keypad.

> "Okay, Doc. Give it to me straight. How bad is it?"

A grin greeted me from across the room. "I want you to spend about three hours a day doing absolutely nothing," she said. Then she waved a hand at the electronic gadget in my lap. "No playing card games on your computer-thingy. No reading. No crosswords. Maybe a jigsaw puzzle. I'll have to think about that—okay, for now. But mainly I want you to sit on your porch and listen to the birds. I want you to give your mind and your brain a rest. Don't write anything, don't tell any jokes, don't cook or clean"—I loved the sound of that—"no leading your Bible study group, no spending hours crying out to God. Just sit. I want you to engage in nothing but absolute brainless activity for a while."

I couldn't resist the setup: "I thought my life was brainless activity!"

She smiled, but I sensed it was only out of kindness. "No jokes, remember? Do you want to come back next week?"

I agreed. And that's how we began our relationship—brainlessly.

To: Chonda
Subject: Accepting medical help
From: Lila

Dear Chonda,

As a pastor's wife who struggles with depression, I have
so appreciated the laughter you have brought me, even
in the darkest times, through your CDs. You have joined
me on many an anguished walk and lifted my spirit often.
You have validated many a woman (especially those in
the so-called foreground of ministry) with your message
that depression is real, and there is nothing wrong with
accepting medical help when it's necessary. I pray that
you find continued encouragement and joy in your life!

In Christ,
Lila

expert
insight

The Shovel and the Pickax

A good therapist asks questions. An excellent therapist asks the hard questions. She faces her client with shovel in one hand and pickax in the other, prepared to dig to the core of the problem and help the depressed person confront issues and put blame where it belongs. Sometimes the therapist coaches the patient to confront whoever caused the grief, if another person was at fault. If the patient is responsible for some of her own problems, the therapist helps her learn to forgive herself. The therapist also helps her put things into perspective: Can this situation be changed? Can anything be done now to change the past?

Unfortunately, it's very common for families to handle traumatic events by not talking about them. The result?

Psychological or emotional crashes in later years. But once the buried past is brought to light, a patient often begins to come out of her depression. She needs that opportunity to be angry or devastated over past events that were emotionally "stuffed" or not confronted. The relief that comes from doing this is palpable, physically and mentally. She becomes empowered, not only to beat her depression, but to change her life.

If you struggle with depression, find a courageous therapist and ask her to bring her shovel and pickax. Enlist her help in digging out and discarding the junk from your past. It will be the best mining you'll ever do—and your tunnel of darkness will turn into life-giving light!

chapter
7

I am now the most miserable man living. If what I feel were equally distributed to the whole human family, there would not be one cheerful face on the earth. Whether I shall ever be better I can not tell; I awfully forebode I shall not. To remain as I am is impossible; I must die or be better, it appears to me.

—Abraham Lincoln

Why are you downcast, O my soul?

Why so disturbed within me?

Put your hope in God, for I will yet praise
him, my Savior and my God.

—Psalm 42:5–6

are we there yet?

I have a list of what I call "God questions"—those hard-to-answer questions I've tucked away for the time when I see God face to face. And, of course, as I get older—see more, hear more, experience more—that list gets longer and longer. Not long ago I did an inventory of my God questions and noticed that the ones that used to be right there at the top have dropped down several notches. I've had to add more pertinent, more immediate questions. Those are the ones on top now.

For a long time my plan, when I first got to heaven, was to hug God's neck, maybe dance around a bit, and then start right in with my questions: "Why did my little sister suffer? Why was Charlotta killed, just when she had found some happiness in her life?"

But lately I've thought I may not start with those questions at all. Some days I look at the world around me, think of my sisters, and say, "Those lucky gals!" I used to get teary-eyed at the thought that they were missing seeing my children grow up. But then I look at Chera Kay, my daughter, and see so much of Cheralyn and Charlotta in her that somehow I know my sisters are very near. I don't think they've missed one minute of my kids' lives.

> "How'd you do it? How'd you keep from whacking all your brothers in the head after they messed with your favorite coat?"

No, those questions about my sisters may be too easy for God. I have bigger ones—ones that I'm sure will make him scratch his head and prompt him to offer me a seat there at his feet while he collects his thoughts.

For example, I want to know: Why giraffes? I mean, I've heard about the long neck being necessary to reach the higher fruit in the treetops and all, but why not put the fruit lower or cause it to drop off whenever a certain creature walks by? That would save on neck material.

And what's with Yellowstone? There are mud pits and thermal pits and pits that smell like rotten eggs and pits that spit and spew, and I can't help but wonder, Is all that spitting and spewing really necessary? Even more amazing, there's a tree in Yellowstone that only reproduces as the result of a forest fire. So something that can be both dangerous and devastating (not to mention awfully hot) is really God's way of exfoliating the mountainside. Isn't there a better way to grow a few trees?

And then I have another whole bag of questions for some of the people I've read about in the Bible. I want to have a long talk with Joseph—not the Joseph-and-Mary Joseph, but the coat-of-many-colors Joe. I want to ask: "How'd you do it? How'd you keep from whacking all your brothers in the head after they messed with your favorite coat?" I mean, I snuck into my big sister's closet and "borrowed" her favorite bell bottoms when I was thirteen, and you'd have thought I had thrown her into a pit and sold her to the Egyptians!

Then there's Paul: "Did you ever get writer's cramp? How many letters did you write that we never got a chance to read? Did your mother ever ask you, 'So you've got time to write the church in Ephesus, but you can't stop long enough to send your mother a birthday card? A simple note, at least, letting me know you're still alive? And when are you going to find a nice Jewish girl and settle down?'"

I have a question for Moses too: "Who was the first person to start whining when you crossed the Red Sea?" I mean, there had to be someone. They were God's chosen people—church folks! And you know whenever two or three church folks are gathered together, someone is going to whine: "I didn't know we were going to have to walk across . . . my sandals are getting muddy . . . Mom, are we there yet? . . . I gotta go to the bathroom."

Great questions, don't you think? The problem is, as my list grows longer and my priorities change, so do the positions of the questions. They shift around, from top to bottom to top again. Some days I'm anxious to pull them all out and get started. Then God reminds me that there's plenty of time. I imagine him nodding and agreeing with me: "Yes, these are all fine questions. Incredible questions. Especially that giraffe one—and I'm giving it some thought already. But for now, you'll have to wait. Just be patient. We'll get to them all soon enough."

Ready, Set—Wait!

I read a little red book not long ago called The Red Sea Rules by Robert Morgan. I figured from the title that it was probably about Moses. And I was right. But I never imagined how much that little red book was about me too.

I continued meeting with my counselor on a regular basis. I had not taken a major "dip" in some time (that's what we people who battle depression call it when we find ourselves heading for bottom—an appropriate term, I think). Our counseling times were mostly times of reflection and learning to let go of things I can't control—like depression, for instance. Much of what my counselor and I discussed I'd heard before and even said before: God loves me, my family loves me; just because things are going great at home doesn't mean I can't be depressed. I knew all this. The drumbeat of all the facts I knew about depression never stopped pounding in my consciousness. But it was nice having someone else's voice, and not just my own, making some of the sound for a while. I was tired of hearing me analyze me, me trying to comfort me, me trying to convince me that everything would be better soon.

We did talk about one thing I hadn't fully considered on my own: my issue with trust. I had to trust God. She grinned when I told her I already knew that.

"And you have to trust yourself," she said. That one stopped me in place.

"And that'll take patience," she added. Which, or course, has never been one of my gifts.

So when I read what Robert Morgan had to say about patience in The Red Sea Rules, I went out and bought lots of copies and gave them to all my friends. If I needed it, then they did too. Here's one of the sections that really got me: "The Red Sea may roll before us; the desert may entrap us; the enemy may press on our heels. The past may seem implausible and the future impossible, but God works in ways we cannot see. He will make a way of escape for his weary, but waiting, children."[1]

Waiting children? But I hate to wait! That's why I'm so grateful for my counselor friend. My times with her made me feel that I was doing something proactive while I was just . . . waiting. From week to week, I waited to see what she would have to say. I waited for the medicine to work. I waited to see whether God would decide to part these waters—or let me drown.

I even wrote across the top of my medicine bottle: "God is working in ways we cannot see. TAKE THE MEDICINE!"

What's Normal?

While I hung out in "God's waiting room" (how many

times have you heard that term and wanted to scream?), my counselor made an appointment for me to see a psychiatrist to reevaluate my medication. You see, counselors and psychologists are incredible professionals to spend time with while you're waiting; but your family doctor or a psychiatrist are the only ones who can write prescriptions and make evaluations about the medicines you may or may not need. And if I might add my personal opinion: you wouldn't make an appointment with a

> I waited for the medicine to work. I waited to see whether God would decide to part these waters—or let me drown.

dermatologist to remove your tooth, would you? Of course not! If a dentist is the best person to pull your tooth and an obstetrician is the best person to deliver your baby, don't you think a psychiatrist might be the best person to check your brain?

After all, he didn't just sit in on a few extra psychology classes in college; he actually went to medical school. He's seen the inside of a brain—and not just in a textbook; he actually dissected brains for real. For him, "body chemistry" isn't a lesson about the compatibility of boys and girls; it's a serious subject to be studied with a microscope, test tubes, and vials of blood and other bodily secretions. Yuck!

As my counselor, she couldn't make the "official" diagnosis on my depression, nor could she write a prescription for my medicine. So when the word bipolar came up in our initial discussions about my family history and seemed to pop up at several subsequent meetings, she wanted to get to the bottom of it. She wanted to make sure that the medication I had been put on initially was really the best choice.

Me? I was still holding out hope for a miracle—or maybe a miracle drug. So I made an appointment with Dr. Haven. Is that not the perfect name for a Christian psychiatrist who is a cross between Santa Claus and the kindest grandfather you could ever imagine? In his office, I felt comfortable. When he prayed, I felt as if I were in a safe . . . uh, haven.

My counselor must have filled him in on my childhood trauma stories, because we didn't spend much time retracing those steps. Instead we talked about my job. He wanted to know how often I worked.

"Not a lot," I said.

He wrote something down and started to ask me the next question, but then I thought of a detail I'd left out. "I mean, we just finished the tour, so I'm not working at all right now."

"Tour?"

"Yeah, we did about eighty-five cities in the last eight months," I said. "But it's over now." I waved a hand to show him how over it was. "So I'm not working at all now."

He wrote something else down.

"Especially since we finished the video."

"Video?"

"Yes, I just shot the video for my next project. We took a crew up to Elkhart, Indiana, did two shows, and recorded them. It went great. All that's over now. I took a vacation right after."

He wrote some more.

"Or at least I started to," I added, suddenly remembering a few more details. "My mom broke her back that weekend, and I had to rush home to take care of her. But she's up and about now. Just as stubborn as ever. So I've got lots of free time."

As he wrote another note on his pad, I remembered one more thing: "I just have to do a final proof on the book, and I'm done."

"You wrote a book?"

"Not a big one. Just a couple hundred pages."

He wrote for a long time then. I imagined Santa Claus making a list and checking it twice. While he jotted his notes, I figured it was as good a time as any to ask, "Do you think I'm bipolar?"

Dr. Haven chuckled (and no, his belly did not jiggle like a bowl full of jelly). "You get right to it, don't you?"

The truth was, it was important to me to know—to hear the official diagnosis. Growing up, I had seen how uncontrolled mood swings in a family member could devastate an entire family. So I had a healthy fear of being bipolar. I had also come to understand that bipolar disorder (also known as manic depression) could be treated

> "Balance is crucial in any life."

and managed with medication. After my initial crash, my family doctor had explained that modern medicine was doing wonders in its effort to cure, alleviate, or at least manage many diseases, including mental illness. Because I had bipolar disorder in my family history, he had placed me on Topamax to go along with my prescription for Zoloft. It was a good call at the time. But now I was ready to go beyond treating the symptoms to getting to the underlying cause. And that meant reevaluating my medicine.

Dr. Haven sat back in his chair and explained that what seemed like manic depression to me could simply be the mania of my job coupled with the reality of a normal life.

Normal? What's that?

"Balance is crucial in any life," he said, "and particularly in the life of a performer."

He didn't have to say another word. I knew exactly what he meant. People ask me all the time, "Are you the same at home as you are on stage?" If by that they mean, do I wear leather pants while scrubbing my bathroom floors, or talk to my family at the dinner table with a microphone, then no. I believe I've discovered a balance there.

What Dr. Haven was suggesting was that I need to expand that balance. Some areas—like how I live on and off-stage—obviously require a certain degree of balance. Other areas are not so obvious. One in particular creeps up on almost everyone in Christian ministry at one time or another: when to work and when to rest.

Uh-oh. We're back to that waiting and patience stuff!

"I don't know if you're bipolar, "Dr. Haven said. "We'll have to wait and see. Let's go ahead and wean you off the Topamax. It's a wonderful medication for helping your body chemistry combat wide mood swings, but that's not where you are right now. We'll continue on the Zoloft for depression. Depression can hang on for quite some time; in fact, sometimes the chemical imbalances in the brain take a lifetime to correct. If you had diabetes, I would be telling you that you're going to be okay as long as you take your insulin to balance your blood sugar levels. So relax and take the Zoloft; it's helping to balance the chemicals in your brain."

He leaned forward and glanced down at his scribbled notes. The he looked up at me. "The mania of your job—the euphoria of having a room filled with people who are laughing and clapping for you—could be misconstrued as a manic episode, especially if you are confusing that euphoria with feeling good, feeling normal. You could be addicted to that," he said. "But you don't show signs of strong manic episodes outside of your performance life. I'm thinking you're just tired and depressed. You must get off the road and stay off the road for a while. That will give us a chance to see exactly what you're normal emotional range is."

There was that word again. What is normal? I mean, I'm around church folks most all the time, and church folks aren't always normal! Church folks can be emotional creatures. I've sat in a pew when the presence of God was so real and so present, it was no wonder that Sister Sarah

Simms was waving a hanky, shouting out loud, and running up and down the aisles. So what if she scared the visitors to death? I thought she was a hoot! I have also sat in a pew when the service was so quiet and reverent—when there was such a sweet, serene calm about God's amazing presence—that I was absolutely moved to tears.

Which was the most authentic experience? I believe one was just as real as the other. After all, God speaks many languages. Just as there are many names to describe God, there are many ways he manifests himself. The Bible teaches us that he is not only El Shaddai (The Almighty), but he is also El Olam (The Everlasting God), El Ohiym (The Strong One), Adonai (Master), and—get this—Yahweh Shalom, which means "The Lord is Peace." (That's one facet of God's personality I need to know a lot better!) He is also Jehovah-Rapha, which means, "The Lord Who Heals," and Jehovah-Hoseenu, "The Lord our Maker."

"If God is my maker, does that mean he made me like this?" I asked my mother one day.

"Absolutely," she said. "You've just worn out some of the parts he made and haven't used the other parts as much."

My mother has no PhD after her name. She barely made it through high school. But she hit the nail on the head. She was talking about balance—or in my case, the lack thereof.

Thankfully, for every season of our lives, for every circumstance we experience, and for every emotion we feel—balanced or not—God has a customized name by which we can call out to him. The key is to take the time to actually call it. I've added a new one to the list. I don't know what the Greek or Hebrew equivalent would be, but I asked my mom about it, and she approves: My God, the One Who Balances Me!

Going to the Funny Farm

According to my counselor and Dr. Haven, my job was to rest. To be patient. To wait. What I needed was to find a cabin in the woods. Someplace where I could get away from the telephone, the commitments, the daily demands—all the things that constantly pulled me into the too-fast lane.

But where could I find a cabin in the woods? Oh, wait. I have a cabin in the woods! A few years ago my husband and I built a quiet place in middle Tennessee, nestled in the rolling hills between the Cumberland and Harpeth Rivers, where pastors and missionaries can go to rest and unwind. The landscape includes seventy acres of trees and a two-acre manmade lake that we "built" and filled with fish. David even constructed a worm bed to breed the kind of slimy, slithery worms that fish love. Who couldn't rest at a place like that? We call it the Funny Farm. What is not-so-funny is that, when my therapist and my psychiatrist prescribed rest, I couldn't remember the last time I'd actually sat on the front porch and rested.

I can almost hear the reporter asking me in VH-1 Behind the Scenes fashion: "So why didn't you just stop and go to the cabin and rest?"

> When my therapist and my psychiatrist prescribed rest, I couldn't remember the last time I'd actually sat on the front porch and rested.

Well, why is it so hard for moms everywhere to take a break? Advertisers encourage women to take some "me-time." "After all, you deserve it," the smooth-talking, silver-tongued voice-overs claim. But the thought of "me-time" sounded absolutely selfish to me. I was already a basket case of guilt because of all the days my job took me away from my kids.

I could just hear Zachary: "Mom, are you going to be here this weekend?"

"Uh, no, Son. I'm going to go away for some 'me-time.' Good luck with supper!"

I just couldn't do it. I completely beat myself up over it. Call me old-fashioned, but I felt that when I was at home, I had to be the mom, wife, cook, cleaner, and chief carpooler (is that even a word?). I cooked big meals, got all the laundry done, and made the dentist appointments, because that's what "good mothers" do. And in my case, it was the least I could do, since I was usually three days away from climbing on a bus and being on the road for a week. "Me-time" was not an option.

But then my sweet Mary—I mean, Doris—reminded me one day: "Chonda, did you know that Jesus had 'me-time'?"

Jesus? The one and only, the Son of God—that Jesus—had "me-time"? It seemed unlikely, and yet I knew it was true. I'd read my Bible. But until Doris posed the question, I'd never made the simple connection—between Jesus and me.

The Lord knew exactly what "needing to get away" felt like and how important it was. He said to his disciples, "Come with me by yourselves to a quiet place and get some rest" (Mark 6:31 NIV). I love the way the Matthew Henry Commentary explains it:

> The tender care Christ took for their repose, after
> the fatigue they had (Mark 6:31); He said unto them,
> perceiving them to be almost spent, and out of breath,

Comeyeyourselvesapartintoadesertplace,andrestawhile. Note, Christ takes cognizance of the frights of some, and the toils of others, of his disciples, and provides suitable relief for both, rest for those that are tired, and refuge for those that are terrified. With what kindness and compassion doth Christ say to them, Come, and rest! Note, The most active servants of Christ cannot bealwaysuponthestretchofbusiness,buthavebodies that require some relaxation, some breathing time; we shall not be able to serve God without ceasing, day and night, till we come to heaven, where they never rest from praising him, Revelation 4:8 . . . The most public persons cannot but wish to be private sometimes.[2]

If Christ rested, then Lord knows my very less-than-divine flesh needed a rest. And so did my emotions! Who knows?Ithought.Maybethisdepressionispartofmydesert. Andifmydesertislikethedisciple'sdesert—ifJesushascalled metoit—thenmaybeI'llhavethesameresultsthedisciples did.Whentheycameout,theysawamiracle:Jesuswalking on water. Who knows? Maybe I'll see a miracle too.

"Okay, okay, okay. I'll rest," I told everyone. I told myself. And so I went to the cabin in the woods to rest—kicking and screaming the whole way.

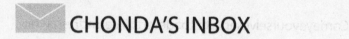 **CHONDA'S INBOX**

To: **Chonda**
Subject: **Thank you for the blessings!**
From: **Nancy**

Dear Chonda,

Thank you for the blessings you have given me by sharing about your depression. I am twenty-two years old, and I have depression. My cousin gave me your DVD, and even though I was as sick as a dog, I watched it. I don't think I have ever laughed so hard in my life! It was so encouraging to know that there are women out there who have depression and talk about it. Thank you for your testimony and your stories. Please don't stop!

Nancy

expert
insight

Rest and Relaxation

It's no accident that the U.S. Armed Forces sends its service members who are in combat areas on what is called "R & R"—"Rest and Relaxation." Our fighting men are under a great deal of stress, fear, and pressure. Taking time away from the battle zone refreshes the bodies and spirits of these brave soldiers and allows them to return, ready to take up the fight again.

The same is true for each of us in our daily battles with life. Sometimes a person can be so overloaded with stress, responsibilities, and commitments that a point is reached where she can no longer cope—where she wants nothing more than to just "check out." This point is often where depression kicks in. Thankfully, this kind of depression can usually be treated with rest and relaxation. Occasionally, though, this point brings to light something else: a pre-existing chemical imbalance that requires antidepressant medication, as well as R & R.

It's okay to take a time-out. It's healthy and refreshing. But make sure that while you're resting, you're not subconsciously beating yourself up for taking time off. And don't use your time to analyze and rehash every mistake you ever made. Here's a better idea: Make a list of activities and responsibilities that you could cut out or delegate to others, thereby freeing up some time for yourself. Do you really have to chair the church supper for the umpteenth time in a row? Do you really have to belong to the book club just to prove that you're a scholar? Do you really have to volunteer at the homeless shelter, when you're already volunteering at the food bank?

It's no big surprise that depression disorders occur twice as often in women as men, since women tend to take on extra responsibilities more often. Be honest with yourself. Do you do these activities because you really want to? Or do you do them because you want to be liked or admired or because you'll feel guilty if you don't?

It's a good trade-off—canceling some obligations in exchange for better mental health. Find ways to have fun. Find ways to give yourself more hours in the day. Not only will you restore your mind and emotions; you will restore your soul.

chapter
8

I've had a wonderful time, but this wasn't it.

—Groucho Marx

Humble yourselves, therefore, under

God's mighty hand, that he

may lift you up in due time; cast

all your anxiety on him

because he cares for you.

—1 Peter 5:6–7

enough
baloney!

I can remember the times in my life when I really messed up—times when I did things I'm not very proud of, things I'm sure made God frown. I can remember them like they were yesterday. Can't get them out of my head sometimes.

I'm not going to write about them now. You won't find details about them anywhere in this book, so don't go flipping ahead looking for juicy tidbits. Fact is, I dealt with those messes and their consequences long ago. They're in the past. Over.

But I can still remember them. That's the point. The times when I messed up are filed away in my brain, and the memory of them is still in there somewhere.

Of course, when you trust Jesus with your life and ask him to forgive you, God wipes your slate clean. You're no longer guilty. He puts your sins as far away as the east is from the west. I know and believe that.

But Satan likes to scamper through your files, scribbling down notes about your past sins and doing whatever he can to draw your attention to them. He pulls out the yellowed pages and flags them with bright colored markers and bold stars in the margins, trying to make you look—to make you remember.

What's worse, he doesn't just stick with your sins; he tries to make you remember the sins of others too. He likes to highlight and underline all the times that you were hurt and shamed by other people's mistakes or bad choices. Added to the pain you bring on yourself, the sins of others give Satan quite an arsenal. It's an almost bottomless cache of weapons designed to keep you reeling when depression strikes—to keep you living as a victimized prisoner of the past. Your past sins and hurts can haunt you until you can

> Your past sins and hurts can haunt you until you can barely stand.

barely stand. I know; I could have written this chapter dozens of times from the floor of my own home.

It's easy for your thinking to get twisted when Satan keeps you focused on sins, mistakes, and painful events. What's hard is uncoiling all those wound-up experiences so that you start thinking straight again. In my case (like most people with clinical depression), I couldn't do it on my own. I needed help from my doctors, my therapist, my friends—and most of all from God.

Belts, Fly Swatters, and Throw Pillows

Before we move on, I feel I must give you a warning like the one you often hear just before a particularly vivid, made-for-TV docudrama: "Some scenes in this chapter may contain graphic material not meant for children." It's the least I can do, because . . . well, my past contains some graphic material.

I'm sure I'm not telling you anything new when I say that your parents are the most influential people in your life. They get you when you're young and mushy and ready to be molded any which way. If they're good parents—yippee! You grow up with fewer coils that have to be unwound

153

down the road. But if they're not so great—if they struggle with major problems of their own—then most likely you grow up looking like a Slinky. And if you don't find a way to break the spiraling cycle that your parents (or your parents' parents) started, you risk revisiting as an adult the pain you suffered as a child. You risk getting tangled up in your own coils.

In my case, I grew up as a preacher's kid. My two sisters, my brother, and I knew about God from the time we could know about anything.

"What's that on your face? Your nose! And where does God live? In heaven! Yeah!"

That was one of the best parts of my childhood. I have believed in God for as long as I can remember. But other parts of my growing-up years were not so good, and they left painful memories in the files in my brain.

For example, in my family there was no such thing as a time-out. Every adult spanked; some just spanked more fiercely than others. My grandmother used to make Mike, Charlotta, Cheralyn, and me find our own switches. One day I searched the privet hedges for an hour. When Grandma poked her head outside to see what was taking me so long, I reported, "Can't find one! Must have used them all!" Don't you know, it took her all of two minutes to search those same hedges and find the perfect switch.

I have an aunt who used a flyswatter. A flyswatter has a very large strike zone. Two swats were equal to a dozen privet hedge switch lashings.

Then there was my mom. She would pick up anything that was nearby and take a swing at us. Most of the time, she grabbed something hilariously ineffective, like a throw pillow from her bed or a dish towel by the kitchen sink. She would swing away until we started laughing, and then she would laugh, and, well . . . it was a given: Mother was a softy!

My father, on the other hand, was anything but. He believed in the power of the belt. And over the course of my childhood, I had enough encounters with his belt to become a believer too.

Dad had an unusual rule when it came to doling out punishment to his kids. When one of us got a swatting, all of us got a swatting. In some inexplicable way, this seemed fair to him. We were put on notice: If you do something wrong, not only will you get a good swatting, but the consequences of your actions will bring harm to those closest to you. Fair or not, I have to say that Dad's method was effective—if a kid crying and begging, "I'm sorry! Just beat me. Please, just beat me" can be considered effective. None of us wanted the others to get spanked for something they didn't do. That threat helped keep us in line most of the time.

But kids are kids, and the belt came out more times than I can count. Most of the time we were made to line up and bend over so that our noses touched the couch cushions. My father would then make us drop our pants, so that the leather was sure to make solid contact with our bare bottoms—a ritual that became more and more humiliating the older we got. As young girls, my sisters and I would make our way to the bathroom after each encounter, wipe our eyes, and compare bottoms, as if we were comparing notes after a math test.

> I don't know when the discipline stopped and the abuse began.

"What answer did you get for number four? Good grief, is that blood?"

I don't know when the discipline stopped and the abuse began. I was almost thirty-five years old the first time I ever told anyone about my father's method of punishment. I can almost guarantee you that my father has never admitted to one moment of abusing anyone. He just doesn't see it that way.

Mike finally stopped it. He was around thirteen or fourteen years old. It's funny; I can remember that last group whipping, but I don't remember what the offense was—I don't even remember which one of us did the dirty deed. But I will never forget the sound of my father's belt making that familiar whoosh as it sliced the air, followed by a slap that I'd never heard before. I dared to look up. To my surprise, the belt was in my brother's grasp. With a sudden movement, Mike had yanked the belt away from my father. His hand must have been stinging. I'm convinced that he completely stopped time. None of us could breathe.

This is the end for Mike, I thought. He won't survive this. But then my brother squared his shoulders, looked Dad straight in the eye, and said, "Enough. We're not doing this anymore. If you want to beat someone, beat me." And my father did. But that was the last time. Ever.

A Dangerous Diet

As I said, I can't tell you when the discipline turned into abuse. Frankly, that's not my point in telling this story. The point is that whatever Dad's intentions were—whatever we were supposed to learn to do or not do—became secondary to the underlying message: My brother, my sisters, and I were connected, and we were responsible for each other.

If Mike, Charlotta, and Cheralyn were in pain, it was probably my fault somehow. I could make their bottoms bleed simply by not eating my carrots.

It's one thing to be taught to be a good sister and to be held responsible for supporting your siblings. A good sister should watch out for her younger sister on the playground and give her a boost up the ladder of the slide. It's another thing to twist that lesson to the point that when an older sister is killed in a car accident or a younger sister dies with leukemia, you think it's your fault. Somehow you failed in your responsibility.

I came out of my childhood and teenage years believing that my wrong choices, my poor judgments, my weaknesses and failures—my sin—were not only the catalyst for the pain that visited and revisited my backside, my head, and my heart; they were also what brought down a host of pain upon the people I loved most. From there it was only a few steps to believing that when the Bible talked about "visiting the iniquity of the fathers upon the children and the children's children to the third and the fourth generation" (Exodus 34:7 NKJV), it meant that I would be forever plagued, not only by what I'd done wrong in the past, but by what my father had done, and what his father had done before him. If they were bipolar (and they were), then I would be bipolar. If they sinned (and they did), then I would pay the price. I would have to keep bending over, touching my nose to the couch cushion, waiting to be punished.

As my own kids grew up, I took my misguided beliefs one step further. I figured that since I had messed things up as a teenager, then I had messed things up for my own teenagers—the ones I loved with my life, the ones I was trying to raise the best I could. It was like some crazy, never-ending, exponentially growing, pyramid-of-sin scheme. In such a hopeless cycle of sin, blame, and feelings of worthlessness, you're defeated before you can even begin.

Baloney!

Of course it is. I know that now. But when you're depressed, you think baloney is filet mignon. You score it, marinate it, and slap it on the grill. But when you finally bite into it, reality sets in (or is it heartburn?) and you realize it ain't steak—it's baloney.

No matter how much you think you know and understand God, depression can bring you to the point where you doubt God, yourself, and your own salvation. You convince yourself that God could not possibly forgive you for the things you have done. Your mind tells you that Elvis is dead and God has indeed left the building. At least, that's what my mind told me—usually right after a lecture from the talking lights.

At some point, though, I realized I needed to lay off the bologna and improve my diet. (Okay, that's the end of the food metaphors—I'm getting hungry!)

Just Hang Up!

Sometimes it's our stinkin' thinkin' that gets us in trouble. You know—one stinkin' thought leads to another, which leads to another, which leads to another. Eventually the smell will kill you!

Breaking the stinkin' thinkin' habit hasn't been easy. I'm still working on it. But over time I came to see that the Bible doesn't support the twisted ideas I learned as a child. The apostle Paul says,

> If anyone is in Christ, he is a new creation; the old has gone; the new has come! All this is from God, who reconciled us to himself through Christ and gave us the ministry of reconciliation: that God was reconciling the world to himself in Christ, not counting men's sins against them. And he has committed to us the message of reconciliation. (2 Corinthians 5:17–19)

What part of "not counting men's sins against them" did I not understand?

Obviously, I needed to take a deep breath and a step back. I needed reconciliation. I needed deliverance. I needed to speak truth to the curses in my past and rebuke the darkness. I needed to hold my head up, stick my chin out, and say, "Baloney!" I needed to stop reading the old files and dive into the Word of God instead.

What I needed was Beth Moore! But since I don't know where she lives, her books had to suffice. In Breaking Free: Making Liberty in Christ a Reality in Life, she writes:

> What part of "not counting men's sins against them" did I not understand?

God does not punish children for their parents' sins. In Exodus 20:5 I believe God says he will be able to review or take a census of all the times the effects of the parents' sins can be seen in the next several generations. He will be able to number those who have been adversely affected by the sins of their parents or grandparents. For instance, if a pollster took a census of the number of alcoholics in three generations of an alcoholic patriarch's family, the head count would very likely be high. Why? Because alcoholism was deposited in the family line. It came calling, and an unfortunate number of children and grandchildren answered the door.[1]

In other words, we have free will. We have a choice. We can refuse to answer the door. We can break the cycle! Children don't have to suffer for their parents' sins. There is hope! Later in that same chapter, Moore explains the true meaning of the passage in Exodus about "visiting the iniquities of the fathers on the children." She says, "I don't believe [God is] calling a curse down on anyone. I believe God is referring to a natural phenomenon placed in poignant words in Hosea 8:7, "They sow the wind and reap the whirlwind." Parents and grandparents must be very careful what they sow, because it may reap the wind in their own lives and the whirlwind in the lives that follow.[2]

In my own life, it was high time for the whirlwind to die.

In chapter 6 I mentioned a woman named Lana Bateman, who travels with Women of Faith as the chaplain for the speakers. She's like Beth Moore, Mother Teresa, and Oral Roberts rolled into one—and when it comes to dealing with Satan, a bit of Muhammad Ali. She can rope-a-dope Satan in a heartbeat! She's a petite, tender lady; but when she prays, she cuts through darkness and reaches closer to the throne of heaven than probably anyone I've ever known.

One day Lana and I had a very matter-of-fact talk about my childhood traumas, my sinful past, and my "cursed" bloodline. Then we prayed—and there was nothing matter of fact about it. That day heaven and earth shook. Satan screamed. And the whirlwind was relegated to a puff. Lana reached out, took the belt in her hand, and said, "Enough. It ends today."

Now I make it a point to tell others who may be struggling with the sins of the past (whether theirs or someone else's): God is in the business of reconciling people to himself. He is in the business of reconciling the past so that it no longer hovers like a dark, swirling cloud over the present and the future.

In Christ there is no condemnation. You're not a Slinky, and neither am I. We're new creatures.

And, oh yeah—Satan is a liar, and depression is his cell phone. Next time he calls, hang up!

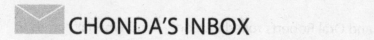

CHONDA'S INBOX

To: **Chonda**
Subject: **Music ministry**
From: **Holly**

Dear Chonda

I saw you last night at the Women of Faith conference and was sorry to hear that you were suffering with depression. I, too, have suffered with this devastating disease. A wonderful sister in Christ from my church told me that she thought I was clinically depressed, so I got professional help. While I was recovering and healing, your music ministry was such a blessing. During my recuperation period, I clung for dear life to your beautiful rendition of "God Loves You." It truly helped me put Satan's lies behind me. And the medication didn't hurt either! Praise God!

Holly

expert insight

"If Only"

Often a depressed person will get a bad case of the "if onlys." "If only my husband hadn't left me." "If only my parents hadn't been killed in that car wreck." "If only I could lose weight." "If only I had been a better mother." "If only _____." You fill in the blank.

If you find yourself saying over and over, "If only _____," stop for a moment and remind yourself that the past is there and then, and there's nothing you can do to change it. Think positively about the here and now, and quit beating yourself up. Here's a little trick to help you: Put a good, thick rubber band on your wrist. Every time you have a negative thought or speak negative, "if only" words, snap the rubber band. Hurt yourself. Be consistent!

This is called behavioral conditioning. Your brain is not stupid; soon it will get the connection between the pain and your negative words or thoughts, and it will stop you whenever you start going down that track.

One more thing about the "if onlys": Never use the "if only" excuse regarding your depression, as in, "If only I weren't depressed, I could . . ." If you've been diagnosed with clinical depression, accept it—and then determine to beat it through prayer, exercise, therapy, medications, and any other tools that your doctor recommends. Spending time in "if only" daydreams will keep you from dealing effectively with the reality of your condition. You need to be focused on doing the things that will bring you back to fullness of health.

chapter
9

If we couldn't laugh, we would all go insane.

—Jimmy Buffet

Where there is no guidance

the people fall,

But in abundance of counselors

there is victory.

—Proverbs 11:14 NASB

peri-normal,
peri-mental, or
peri-menopause?

Over the course of my stay at the Depression Hotel, I met with all kinds of medical and mental health specialists—emergency-room doctors, family doctors, surgeons, psychologists, therapists, psychiatrists, you name it. If they had a degree after their name, I probably had an appointment with them at one time or another. But there was one kind of doctor I hadn't thought to consult until some friends brought up the idea.

I have a wonderful group of friends who meet at my house for Bible study on Tuesday nights. Except for the short hiatus we took when my counselor pulled the plug so that I could spend all my time bird watching, we've met together faithfully. We call ourselves the Iron Maidens. No, we don't sit around and listen to heavy-metal music! We got the name from Proverbs 27:17: "As iron sharpens iron, so one man"—or woman—"sharpens another." My first thought was to call our group the Buns of Steel, but my pastor nixed that idea. Where's his sense of humor?

> Jesus you can come now. Beth Moore spoke my name!

The Iron Maidens are Beth Moore junkies. We just love Beth's books and Bible studies! So much so, in fact, that after Mike and Doris moved to Tennessee, he and my husband gave Doris and me special bracelets engraved with the letters WWBS ("What Would Beth Say?"). Apparently they were a bit tired of us bringing Beth to every dinner table and on every double date. My brother teases me that I have more Beth Moore quotes memorized than I do Bible verses. He's probably right. In our house it's, "Oprah who?"

The Iron Maidens have traveled far and wide to hear Beth Moore. Once when I was performing in Orlando at a large gathering, the Iron Maidens came along—not to support their fearless leader (me), but to hear Beth Moore, who was on the speakers list. I hate to sound like a silly fan or a groupie or something, but I have to tell you what happened. Beth was introduced right after I finished my performance. As she got ready to start her teaching, she interrupted herself, stepped to one side of the stage, looked over at our little group, and chuckled favorably about what she'd just heard come out of my mouth. Well, that was it. Jesus you can come now. Beth Moore spoke my name! My friends and I giggled and laughed and clutched each other, as if Elvis had just tossed us his sweaty scarf.

I'm Too Young for This!

I am convinced that this group of ladies—the Iron Maidens—were sent to me by divine design. Most of us were strangers when we started meeting. Few had any idea what I did for a living. These women aren't my fans; they're my friends. They have prayed for me and with me. They have fussed at me and encouraged me. And they have provided me with an unending supply of opinions—a fact that probably doesn't thrill my doctors. There's no telling how many times I've started a conversation with one of my doctors with the phrase, "The other day one of my girlfriends said she'd read (heard, saw, or experienced) . . ."

Not long ago, Liz asked me—no, maybe it was Joyce

chapter 9

Ann—on second thought, I'm sure it was Sonia . . . or maybe Tammy . . . let's just say, someone asked me, "Have you been to your gynecologist to see if your struggles with depression have anything to do with menopause?"

I almost slapped her! "I'll have you know, sister, I am only forty-three!"

Someone else chimed in: "So? Haven't you heard of perimenopause?"

"What's that?"

Bad question. We ate up at least twenty minutes of "Beth time" searching the Internet for menopause facts, home remedies, and recipes that included soy milk. That night, iron sharpened iron. We knew, of course, that menopause was a normal stage in a woman's life. Some of us were closer to that stage than others. But what some of us didn't know was that in the lead-up to menopause—a transition period called perimenopause—women go through physical and emotional changes that can sometimes throw everything else in their lives out of whack.

Physical and emotional changes . . . out of whack. That pretty much described the previous ten months of my life! So the next morning I dusted off the old address book and found the phone number for my OB/GYN.

Honestly, I wondered if he was still living. At that

point, I hadn't been to see the OB/GYN in quite a while. I know, I know—getting an annual exam is important. I guess I just didn't feel a pressing need, since the OB part of his title was no longer necessary. I wasn't pregnant. That would have been nearly impossible, since David . . . well, you know.

Besides, I do have a "breast health" doctor I see regularly—ever since I had a lump biopsy a while back. I love this woman; she saved my mother's life several years ago (Mom had been diagnosed with breast cancer). So I make it a point to take her cookies or candy when I see her each year. And I do try to make occasional "pit stops" with out-of-town doctors when I'm on the road. I'm the only gal I know who gets her PAP results from a long distance phone call.

But enough with the excuses. I finally tracked down the phone number of the old OB/GYN office and learned that, since my last visit, my doctor had moved his practice—and retired. And to think he hadn't called me or consulted with me about either decision! So I made an appointment with a new gynecologist in the new office.

I arrived right on time. When I walked in, I couldn't help but notice the lovely, updated décor and that unmistakable "new office" smell. Wow, my two pregnancies must have really helpedthedoctorsprucethingsup!Ithoughttomyself.How could he retire after moving into such great digs?

I signed in as the woman at the reception desk dusted off a file sitting on her desk.

"I had the hardest time finding this," she said. "It's been a while since you've seen the doctor, hasn't it?"

Istartedtodiveintoalitanyofexaggeratedexplanations aboutmywork,mytraveling,myhecticlifestyle;butbefore I got very far, a nurse stuck her head into the waiting room and announced, "Mrs. Pierce, you can come on back."

There Must Be a Better Way

I don't consider myself a celebrity, especially when I'm in my hometown. But every now and then, when I walk into a restaurant, a low buzz will start up somewhere, and I'll notice a few folks staring and whispering; then grinning, pointing, and whispering; and finally someone will nudge someone else, and a gal will walk my way with an ink pen in her hand and . . . take my order!

Ha! Had you going, didn't I?

Actually, every once in a while, a woman will approach me and say, "Are you who I think you are?" Now there's a loaded question! Most of time I answer, "I don't know. Who do you think I am?" And, nine times out of ten, the minute I speak, she screams and calls back to her friends, "I knew it was her! I knew it!" I try to be as nice as possible. I exchange pleasantries and sign napkins for relatives, while my kids stare at me with that all-too-familiar smirk that says, "How many times have we told you not to open your mouth in public?"

This time, as I followed the OB/GYN nurse back to the examination room, I noticed whispering—but I was pretty sure it wasn't the restaurant-variety. Three ladies clad in medical garb were looking over my chart and muttering under their breaths.

They probably can't believe that someone would wait fifteen years to see a gynecologist, I thought.

> I signed in, as the woman at the reception desk dusted off a file sitting on her desk.

I entered the exam room, slipped into one of those luxurious gowns they give you (in fifteen years, that hasn't changed), climbed onto the, uh, recliner (and, by the way, the "cup holders" are still in a very awkward position), and then stared at the new ceiling tiles and light fixtures while I waited.

Finally, in walked the doctor. The doctor? He looked more like the doctor's kid! I mean, how do med schools get away with churning out such young graduates? You know a doctor is fresh out of school, not just because his lab coat is crisp and clean, but because he rolls around on the stool like he's at Disney World.

Oh yeah—this is why I haven't been to see the OB/GYN in a while, I thought. I had to wait until my doctor was potty trained.

As Dr. Junior began the exam, I kept my mind busy by asking questions. "Where did you go to med school? Oh? My daughter is applying there. Do you know anything about something called perimenopause? Is there really such a thing?"

And then it happened. Doctor Junior zipped back on his stool as if he had discovered . . . I don't know what. Then he leaned over so that his head was no longer between my knees, looked directly into my face, and said, "Wait! Are you who I think you are? I've seen you on TV." And then he yelled down the hall, "Louise, you were right! Come in here! Margaret, yep! It's her."

Suddenly I had an audience—but no clever comeback came to mind. I was so flustered, I couldn't even remember jokes I'd been telling for twenty years. Do you know they have a blood test to tell whether or not you're in menopause? Why couldn't I have asked for a do-it-yourself test kit and saved myself the humiliation of signing autographs with my knees in the air and my feet in the "cup holders"?

Finally the exam was finished. All that was left was to endure the blood test.

"Some people in the medical community don't talk much about perimenopause," Dr. Junior told me. "But I wouldn't discount it in your case. It may have something to do with what's going on."

Then he just had to add, "My mom took quite a while to get through the whole process of menopause." Great. A "momma story" from my gynecologist. "So you definitely could be heading there."

Heading there? If you need more conclusive evidence, why don't you come and swab the sweat off my couch!

"By the way," he continued, while I held my tongue, "I noticed on your chart that you're taking Zoloft. My mom took Zoloft too, and it seemed to do wonders for her. I have some samples here I could give you. It'll save you some money. It's the least I can do." Then he grinned, handed me his doctor pen, and added, "Could I get your autograph for my mother?"

When I finally gathered my clothes and scurried out of the office, I made a firm decision to wait another fifteen years before my next visit to the OB/GYN.

chapter 9

A few days later, I got a call from Doctor Junior's office. The blood test had come back "inconclusive." So I'm not in menopause. That's a big help, I thought. But then I smiled. At least my baby-boy gynecologist had recognized perimenopause as a real phenomenon and a possible factor in my roller-coaster of a mental, physical, and emotional state. I took some comfort in that. I also took comfort in the knowledge that Dr. Junior's mother survived her menopause ordeal and eventually became comfortable in her own skin again. Today she's happy, healthy—and hopefully enjoying her five new Chonda Pierce DVDs.

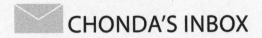

CHONDA'S INBOX

To: **Chonda**
Subject: **Keeping it real!**
From: **Patricia**

Hi Chonda,

I want you to know that your ministry in concert, music, and books has been such a blessing to me! I feel as if you and I were childhood friends because of our common background, losses, and upbringing. I'm going through the hormonal changes, the hot flashes, and the emotional roller coaster. Thank you for helping me laugh about it and for keeping it real! Your willingness to be transparent is much appreciated.

Patricia

expert
insight

What's Perimenopause?

Most women know to expect menopause. They recognize that at some point, typically when they're in their fifties, their ovaries will stop producing eggs, and their menstrual cycles will cease. What fewer women know, however, is that perimenopause can begin eight to ten years before menopause, as their estrogen levels begin to gradually decline. Like menopause and postpartum depression, the hormone changes in perimenopause can significantly affect a woman's mood.

According to the Cleveland Clinic Health Information Center (www.clevelandclinic.org), perimenopause can have some or all of the following symptoms:

- Hot flashes

- Mood swings

- Breast tenderness

- Worsening of premenstrual syndrome

- Decreased libido (sex drive)

- Fatigue

- Irregular periods

- Difficulty sleeping

If you're in your thirties or forties and you're struggling with a depressed mood, it's valid to ask your doctor, "Is it perimenopause, or is it clinical depression?" The proper diagnosis is important; because even though the symptoms for both conditions are similar, the treatment options are completely different. If your depression is caused by a hormonal imbalance or thyroid deficiency, for example, your doctor is likely to recommend hormone replacement therapy or thyroid enhancers, either of which would be totally inappropriate for treating clinical depression.

chapter

10

Do, or do not. There is no "try."

—Yoda

The weapons we fight with are not the

weapons of the world.

On the contrary, they have divine power
to demolish strongholds.

We demolish arguments and every

pretension that sets itself up against the

knowledge of God,

and we take captive every thought to

make it obedient to Christ.

—2 Corinthians 10:4–5

maintain,
maintain,
maintain!

Never let your sixteen-year-old son know you're frightened of lizards. I made that mistake, and since then I've had various shapes and sizes of the wiggly reptiles planted on my shoulders, flung onto my lap, and tucked away under my bed covers. Rational, grownup conversations with my teenage son did not bring an end to this. Neither did the threat of grounding, actual grounding, or an hour-long headlock over a plate of broccoli.

So I decided to take control of my fears. I got me a BB gun. And now I know what Zachary is afraid of: a mom who's "packing"!

I bought the BB gun to shoot at lizards and anything

else that looks vaguely like a lizard—snakes, twigs, twine, algae caught in a current. When I'm hiking or canoeing, anything that wiggles gets shot—or shot at, anyway. The trouble is that once I spot a lizard (or any of the aforementioned wiggly things), I'm shaking so much that it's impossible to aim. So to make up for my lack of precision, I lay down a heavy cover of fire. This sends my husband and kids ducking for safety—in poison ivy, if necessary. Being itchy is better than getting bitten by a snake or mowed down by Mom's BB gun. It's the price they pay for the battle I've chosen to wage against the reptiles of middle Tennessee.

> Truth is, I haven't had to fire the gun in so long, I really don't know if it still works.

Our family lives on a beautiful, winding river, and almost every afternoon my husband and I step out onto the back porch and survey the landscape. David stretches, scratches his belly, and says, "Think I'll drop a hook in, Ma." I, having nothing better to do, say, "Yep. Think I'll drop a hook in with ya, Pa." (Romantic, isn't it?) Ever since I started "packing," I've been more willing to go fishing. I don't worry so much about snakes or lizards down by the water's edge.

Lately, though, I've noticed that rust is forming around the moving parts of my BB gun. And if I tilt the barrel the wrong way, BBs fall out. That never used to happen. Truth is, I haven't had to fire the gun in so long, I really don't know if it still works. But that doesn't stop me from strapping it on when I head down to the water, my hand rested on its plastic grip. It's comforting to know that, at the very least, I can heave the rusty thing at any lizard that dares to cross my path.

The other day my would-be-doctor-daughter laughed at the sight of me marching down to the river like Wyatt Earp to the OK Corral. "There goes Mom with a placebo on her hip!" she said.

I turned back and cocked my head ever-so-slightly. "Are you sure it's a placebo?" I said. "Maybe you should say hello to my little friend!" I patted the barrel, and two BBs dropped out and landed on the ground next to me. I quickly covered them with my foot. Placebo indeed, I thought.

Something—or Nothing?

Have you ever wondered how medicine works—specifically, medicine that is supposed to take care of your mind? That it all baffles me is an understatement. The one thing I'm sure of is that a clinically depressed person needs more than a placebo. Depression may be in the mind, but it's not in the imagination.

Dr. Haven talked to me briefly about how doctors treat depression with medication, and Dr. Alison explained it in more depth. Generally speaking, finding the right medicine for a particular person is a matter of trial and error. Some prescriptions are written as "practice swings." You see, no definitive blood test exists (yet) for identifying depression or bipolar disorder or any other mental illness—unlike, say, diabetes. For mental-health professionals, the diagnosis becomes "educated speculation," and finding the right medicine can mean trying a few that aren't right first.

I know that probably discourages (or downright ticks off) all of the get-it-right-the-first-time people out there. But if there were any other way to diagnose and treat depression or other illnesses of the mind, some very, very, very, very rich doctor would have already come up with it—which would explain, of course, why he was very, very, very, very rich.

So let's say you're bipolar, which means you have mood swings that go from manic to depressive. But in your case, the symptoms on the manic side are so miniscule that depression is the only obvious indicator. So your doctor diagnoses depression and starts you on an antidepressant.

Now, there is quite an assortment of antidepressants on the market. Based on the variety in color and shape alone, if you put one of each pill in a single box, you'd have something that looked like one of those create-a-beaded-necklace kits from the craft store. Some of the pills have a component that helps anxiety-based depression. Some seem to work better for men, others for women. But let's say that in your case, no single color or shape is working. So your doctor adds a prescription for a mood stabilizer; and all of a sudden, everything in your life comes together. Aha! Now you and your doctor know you're not simply depressed; you're bipolar.

This process can work in the opposite direction, as well: The doctor suspects you're bipolar, so he tries a mood stabilizer. But it doesn't help. The conclusion, then, is that you don't have bipolar disorder; you're depressed. Many times psychiatrists will try different medicines first and then make the diagnosis according to which meds work. The bottom line is that when it comes to diagnosing certain mental illnesses, what you might expect to be a precise scientific procedure is actually . . . well, a bit of a guessing game.

Does that make you want to throw up your hands and quit—or stay locked and loaded?

Quitting is tempting, and a lot of people do it. But to me, doing something is always better than doing nothing.

Remember, I'm the woman who heads to the river with a rusty, BB-leaking placebo on her hip. And despite all the uncertainty surrounding my illness, there was one thing I knew for sure: Something was wrong, and I needed help.

The thing is, when you're floundering in the darkness of depression, you need a reason to hope. You need to feel as if you're doing something—even if that something is figuring out what won't work. I mean, think of Thomas Edison. He tried over a thousand different elements before he discovered the right one to use for a light-bulb filament. When asked how he felt about those first thousand or so failures, he responded, "If I find ten thousand ways something won't work, I haven't failed. I am not discouraged, because every wrong attempt discarded is often a step forward."[1]

The only other choice is to do nothing at all, and that's just hopeless. If Thomas Edison had chosen to do nothing, we would all be sitting in the dark!

Calling All Experts

Have you ever noticed that when you suddenly find yourself in a new and different situation, "experts" seem to come out of the woodwork? For example, the first time I was pregnant, people I didn't even know came up to me and gave me lists of the best colleges for my yet-unborn child. Others gave me advice on how to make her smarter by playing classical music over my belly (keep in mind, the only portable option for playing music back then was a boom box). And then there were the folks who said I absolutely must tape a quarter to her belly-button the moment she was out of the delivery room.

The same thing happened when my "new and different situation" was depression. "Experts" popped up everywhere with all kinds of interesting ideas to share. Here's a piece of advice: Don't bother sleeping with a Bible strapped to your head. It doesn't work. My sister-in-law said she read somewhere that Beth Moore slept with the Bible on her head one night. I don't know if it pulled her out of a heavy depression. It just gave me a terrible headache!

One day I heard David Feherty, a golf announcer, talk on TV about his own struggle with depression. Referring to the now-infamous interview between Matt Lauer and movie-star Tom Cruise on NBC's Today Show, Feherty made this comment: "Tom Cruise said there is no such thing as depression. Exercising would make people feel better. I think he is right. I'd like to beat up Tom Cruise. That is exercising, and it would make me feel better!"

I nearly fell off the couch laughing—and I needed the laugh.

It was bad enough when other people thought they were experts about my condition. It got worse when I decided that I was my own number one expert. I figured, I've been down the long, hard road of experience. I've learned what works and what doesn't work. I have lots of good advice to share with other people about depression. I should probably write a book!

Honestly, if I had written this book earlier, it would be missing this one valuable chapter—the chapter about how I nearly destroyed everything. I had to learn the hard way that I was not the expert I thought I was. I was in no position to self-medicate—to make the call about whether or not to take my medicine.

But that's exactly what I did.

"I think I'm cured," I told my husband one day. "I've been exercising—well, walking at least. And I feel really good. No dark, heavy cloud perched on top of my head.

No cell phone ringing in my ear." And with that, I stopped taking my little blue pills.

I told Alison a few days later. All she said was, "Uh-huh. And what does your doctor think about this?"

I waited until a good day to tell Dr. Haven—a really good day, when I had lots of energy in my voice, and confidence just bubbled out of me.

"You know," I told him over the phone, "I think I'm ready to get off the medicine. I'm down to fifty milligrams. That's such a teeny, tiny amount. And besides, I feel great. Really great! I'm ready to get back to the way things were before my crash."

If it were possible to hear a grin, I'm sure I would have heard one coming from Dr. Haven. He responded with the same tone Alison used.

"Uh-huh. And what does David think about this?" Good grief! Doesn't anyone give definitive answers anymore?

His next words surprised me. "Well, it sounds as if you've made your decision," he said. "It's up to you. Go ahead. Just call me in a few weeks and tell me how you're doing."

Something not right here, I thought. Isn't the the expert? Shouldn't the decision about my medication be up to him?

Later I discovered what he really meant (but didn't

say) was, "Go ahead. Strap on your rusty BB gun, if that will make you feel safe. Let's just see what happens when a lizard comes along—and all your BBs have fallen out of the barrel."

A Sinking Feeling

What Dr. Haven didn't know was that I was about to leave for the Holy Land, and David and Alison were going with me. In Israel, I figured, I would be more than covered by light; I would be surrounded by it. In the birthplace of the Light, there would be no room for darkness.

The Holy Land in July is hot. We toured through the holy sites in awe, crying when we were blessed, laughing when we were overwhelmed with joy—and sweating most all the time. Alison had never been to Israel and I had, so I was constantly telling her what to expect around the next corner, up the next street, or in the next town.

I admit it: I'm a terrible person to watch a movie with—especially when I've seen it before. If a funny scene is coming up I will say something like, "Oh, this funny. Watch this." Or if a scary scene is next, I'll cover my eyes and say, "Can't watch this. Too scary!" Friends who have never seen the movie get upset with me. I was the same way with Alison in Israel. "Oh, the Sea of Galilee is just around this corner." "Look! Shepherd's Field!" "Get ready for Jerusalem, you're going to love this!" (In my defense, I probably would have kept my mouth shut more if our guide hadn't been so slow.)

At one point we boarded a wooden boat and sailed onto the Sea of Galilee. The Golan Heights rose to the north, the Judean hills to the south. From previous trips I recognized Tiberius, Capernaum, and the Mount of Beatitudes. David was at the bow talking with some of the men. Minutes before, Alison and I had been giggling like schoolgirls over the trinkets we had purchased in a shop in Tiberius. Now we sat quietly as the wind—the very breath of God—blew across the waters, and tame, rhythmic waves lapped gently against the wooden planks.

"Go ahead. Strap on your rusty BB gun, let's just see what happens when a lizard comes along—and all your BBs have fallen out of the barrel."

That's when that sneaky lizard showed up. I couldn't have been more surprised. My heart clutched as it recognized the all-too-familiar threat. I reached for my BB gun—but it wasn't there. A tear leaked out of my eye. I didn't know how or why, but I was certain it was happening: I was sinking on the Sea of Galilee.

Someone asked me a question, and I snapped-to long enough to answer, "I believe we're having falafels at the kibbutz." Shortly after that, we climbed off the boat. My feet were back on dry land—but I still had the overwhelming sensation that I was going under.

I should have spoken up. I should have talked to David. I knew not to talk to Alison. She's pretty tender and compassionate with most folks, but with me? She knows me too well! Instead of saying sweetly, "Oh, I'm so sorry. Do you think you should have stayed on your meds?" she would have knocked me over the head with the nativity set she bought in Tiberius. So I tucked away my unholy secret and didn't tell a soul. I went on with the trip with that slimy lizard weighing heavily on my shoulders.

A fine time not to be packing, I thought.

I tossed and turned through my remaining nights in the Holy Land. I spent some time in prayer—lots of time in prayer—in every chapel in Israel, as a matter of fact! I walked upon the very ground where Jesus had walked. Yet there remained a heavy gnawing inside me—a sad, aching feeling that something wasn't right inside my head. The darkness was back.

The flight from Tel Aviv to New Jersey is about twelve hours long. That part of the return trip wasn't so bad, really. I just wanted to sleep. (Remember chapter 2?) By the time I made it home—well, let's just say that my nice, dark, quiet bedroom looked a little too inviting. A full-blown wave of depression had rolled in, and I was sloshing around in it good. I felt incredibly defeated—cheated, even, out of the joyous miracle I had thought was mine a few weeks earlier.

I opened my medicine cabinet and, with a sense of bitterness, took out my prescription bottle. It still contained all the little blue pills I should have been taking over the previous few weeks. I screwed off the cap, shook two pills into my palm, tossed my head back, and took my medicine—again.

The next day I called Dr. Haven. After that, I went to speak with my pastor.

"What went wrong?" I asked Pastor Allen.

He gave me the same answer that I often get from him: "I don't know."

"What about my promise?" I protested. "What about all my hard work? What about Jeremiah 32:27: 'I am the Lord, the God of all mankind. Is anything to hard for me?' Well? Am I just too hard for God?"

I went on and on with my questions and protests, while Pastor Allen nodded and listened patiently. Finally I came to a stop (only because I began to blubber), and he had a chance to speak.

"Maybe now it's time to just shut up, listen to the coach, and play the game."

"If you and I knew everything God was doing, we'd be God," he said. "And frankly, I'm not brave enough to make that claim, are you?" (I was thinking!) "Chonda, we've prayed about this. You've done a great job getting all the bases covered spiritually, mentally, and physically. Maybe now it's time to just shut up, listen to the coach, and play the game."

What my pastor—who also happens to be a big sports junkie—meant was, "Do what the doctors say. Work the program. Healing is on the way—just not today."

Not good enough, I declared to myself.

"Why me? Why now? What is God trying to teach me? And why like this?" I cried. I'm not sure what the world record is for the greatest number of questions asked in a fifteen-minute span, but I could very well be the holder of that one. My pastor, on the other hand, could very well hold the record for the shortest answer to so many questions:

"God only knows," he said.

And of course, he's right. We don't know much of anything, do we? My guess is that many of you are about to shut this book and toss it against the wall. Don't feel bad; I've thrown it across three rooms in my house already— and that was long before I ever got to this chapter. You've invested a great amount of time reading through to this point. Maybe you've kept at it because you're fighting your own battle with depression, and you're desperate to find an answer. The truth is that sometimes there is no answer—at least, no single answer.

We want the quick fix, the right prayer, the divine touch, the anointed verse, the piece of holy ground to kiss—or at least the perfect pill. We want to find that one thing that works so that we can say, "Okay, now I can get back to what I was doing before everything got so heavy and dark."

But maybe there is no quick fix, no single step to overcoming depression. Maybe the remedy is a combination of small steps over time—praying, exercising, eating right, getting counseling, taking medicine, following doctor's orders. All of these things contribute greatly to the healing process, some more than others. Who knows which one works best—or when?

I know, I know—God does.

Recently my pastor said something that was very wise. "Good health is not something you obtain, it's something you maintain," he told me—and that goes for mental health, physical health, and spiritual health. "For example, what I did in the gym when I was in high school means nothing to me today," he explained. "If I don't maintain, I wind up having to lose the same ten pounds over and over." According to Pastor Allen, we never finish being healthy. We have to keep working to maintain our health, using whatever tools God has put at our disposal.

He added, "When someone tells me that they've dealt with their past demons already, I want to ask, 'So what are you doing today?'"

What does that mean for those of us who struggle with depression? It means that starting to feel healthy again is not a reason to stop working at being healthy. It's not a reason to throw away all the tools God gave us to get to that point. We keep praying. We keep exercising. We keep taking the medicine if we need it. We don't stop; we maintain.

Winning the War, Not Just the Battle

My church has a wonderful resource center filled with great books. Over the years I have read many of them. I love Max Lucado. I read everything that John Ortberg writes. But one book in particular has really spoken to me in my battle with depression: Blessings and Curses by Derek Prince.[2] Derek was a well-known pastor, Bible teacher, and author who passed away in 2003. He was also someone who struggled with depression.

When I first heard that, I was shocked. After all, he was a respected Christian leader and a modern pioneer in the area of deliverance ministry. Derek Prince—depressed? It was hard to imagine. But then I picked up Blessings and Curses and began to wrestle through many of its passages. I also began talking to people about the possibility of my own need for deliverance. And I have to tell you, the process was, well . . . a blessing and a curse! (I just had to throw that in. I crack myself up sometimes!)

You know by now that I had a tough childhood. But the trouble didn't start there. Trace my heritage back a few centuries, and you will understand why I was fearful of the past affecting my present. I'm not sure everything that happened within my family tree was demonic. But if Satan himself is at the root of all evil, then demonic pretty well describes a lot of what went on.

You have to understand, I wasn't afraid of submitting myself to deliverance ministry. I believe that through prayer we can be delivered from the curses of the past and receive the blessings that are our inheritance as new creatures in Christ. But I thought I'd already done that. "My fear," I told a friend at church, "is that I am still being visited by the demons of my past—even the past I thought I had been delivered from."

My friend, who also read Blessings and Curses, replied, "It's one thing to be delivered; it's another thing altogether to stay delivered."

She was paraphrasing Derek Prince—and she was right. No matter how we interpret or approach the "blessings and curses" issues from our pasts, the fact is, once we invite God into our lives and he sets our minds free from demonic pressure, we must begin the process of re-education. We must begin to cultivate a different outlook and a new way of thinking. That kind of mind renewal is impossible before we're delivered. But after we're delivered, it's not only a possibility; it's our responsibility.

Thankfully, God has provided everything we need—first to protect our minds from satanic attack, and then to begin the process of renewing our minds. Ephesians 6:14–18 lists six key pieces of equipment that he's put at our disposal: the girdle of truth, the breastplate of righteousness, the shoes of the preparation of the gospel of peace, the shield of faith, the helmet of salvation, and the sword of the Spirit—all made effective through the weapon of prayer.

In the battle against depression, the helmet of salvation is especially important. It's also called the helmet of hope, and it's made to cover our heads—to protect our thought lives. I'm no soccer player, but even I know that a couple of good shin guards won't help much when the ball is coming right for your noggin! Only a helmet will do. With our helmets on, Satan's negative thoughts can't hurt us. We're free to learn how to think in a new and more positive way.

> We must begin to cultivate a different outlook and a new way of thinking.

There's an old song I hear from time to time on a commercial. Patti LaBelle is singing it in the background, while her dubbed-over voice talks about her struggle with diabetes. (Yes, thanks to modern technology, Patti can sing and talk at the same time!) I can't tell you what product the commercial is hawking, because I'm always too busy singing along to notice: "I got a new attitude!"

Once when I was singing along with Patti, it hit me: That's exactly what I need. I didn't need more deliverance; I needed to stay delivered by developing a new mindset—a new attitude. Romans 12:1–2 says,

> I urge you, brothers, in view of God's mercy, to offer your bodies as living sacrifices, holy and pleasing to God—this is your spiritual act of worship. Do not conform any longer to the pattern of this world, but be transformed by the renewing of your mind. Then you will be able to test and approve what God's will is—his good, pleasing and perfect will.

Putting Derek Prince, Ephesians 6, and Romans 12 together really opened my eyes. I told my husband, "I never want to go back to the way things were before I got depressed. I want to be better. I want to re-learn some things, re-think some issues. I want to be changed, transformed. I want a new attitude."

Of course, he was all for it.

I don't know a lot about Derek Prince's fight with depression or his views on treatment options. Now that he's with Jesus, I can't ask him, "What do you think about Tom Cruise?" Or more specifically, "What is your view on Christians and antidepressants?" I hope his answer would be a lot like Pastor Allen's: "Do exactly what the doctor tells you, and do exactly what Scripture tells you. And quit asking which came first, the chicken or the egg. Develop your relationship with the one who created them both."

What I do know is that Derek Prince believed that achieving and maintaining a healthy mind is not a single battle, but an ongoing war. And in a war, you need more than a rusty old BB gun on your hip.

Yes, I had spent some time fighting. In fact, I had spent months and months fighting, doing all the right things—all the necessary and important things—to beat my depression. But then, when the battlefield noise leveled off, I had put down my weapons, figuring the fighting was done. Big mistake.

When your mind has been captivated by the dark for a long time and you finally experience some healing—whether instantaneously through an act of God or gradually through the gift of medicine—you feel liberated. It's an exhilarating feeling. But it's not the end. There's more work to be done. It's like having any other serious, debilitating illness or injury. You're excited when you make it through all the surgeries, but you still have to battle through rehabilitation in order to learn to walk, talk, and feed yourself again.

Now I knew what I had to do: offer my body as a living sacrifice. That would be my spiritual act of worship. Then I had to put on my helmet of hope, start renewing my thinking, and get back in the war.

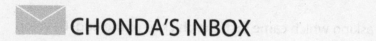

CHONDA'S INBOX

To: **Chonda**
Subject: **Depression is an illness**
From: **Shirley**

Hey Chonda!

I just wanted to say thanks for being so forthcoming about your struggle with depression. I suffered from major depression for many years and never felt the liberty to share that with my brothers and sisters in Christ. I have been told, "You can't be a Christian if you have depression!" Thanks for bringing depression into the light as an illness. Maybe it will help people to accept it as such and not be so critical of those who are experiencing it.

Shirley

expert
insight

Don't Be a Quitter!

A thorn in the side of every psychologist is the patient who decides she has overcome her depression and quits—quits taking her medication, quits exercising, quits watching her diet, quits going to therapy. Before long, she's back to square one, back in the therapist's office, wondering what went wrong.

There's a simple answer: she quit too soon. When a depressed person starts feeling better, she often thinks she no longer needs her meds, her therapy, or her depression-fighting routine. Nothing could be further from the truth. This is a critical point in her recovery. What got her to this point may very well be necessary to keep her there.

Medication may be needed for many more months—

maybe even for the rest of her life, if a chemical imbalance is at the root. A diabetic wouldn't quit taking insulin just because her blood counts were scoring normal, would she? Exercise, which releases endorphins in the brain that elevate mood and produce a sense of well-being, is still important. So is a good diet that keeps the immune system strong and reduces stress on the body.

Your doctor or therapist will know when, or if, it's time to taper off your antidepressant medication and stop your therapy sessions. But hopefully, eating well and exercising regularly will become lifestyle changes that you will continue for the rest of your life. Both are important for lifelong mental and physical health.

chapter
11

Although the world is full of suffering,
it is full also of the overcoming of it.

—Helen Keller

I still belong to you; you are holding my

right hand. You will keep on guiding

me with your counsel, leading me to a

glorious destiny. Whom have I in heaven

but you? I desire you more than anything

on earth. My health may fail, and my spirit

may grow weak, but God remains the

strength of my heart; he is mine forever.

—Psalm 73:23–26

the master puzzler

My brother is a recovering addict, so I know about Alcoholics Anonymous meetings. At AA meetings, the chairs are always in a circle. When people take their seats, the new guys are always a little shy. They hang their heads a little lower and their voices shake a little more than everyone else's. Yeah, you can always spot the newbies.

Imagine you're sitting in a circle with me. Not at an AA meeting, but something like it. I go first. I stand shyly and say, "Hi my name is Chonda."

"Hi, Chonda," the room replies.

Then I begin my confession. "I'm a puzzler," I say, my

head bowed and my voice cracking. "That's right; you heard me. I work puzzles."

Now I don't know if a strong desire to put puzzles together can be called an addiction. But I do love working puzzles. I know, I know—puzzle working sounds like an activity for little old ladies sipping cups of warm tea and chatting about FDR in the sunroom of the retirement home. But just because your grandmother is the last person you saw sitting down working a puzzle doesn't mean that someone like me can't find an almost addictive joy and serenity in the effort to put a puzzle together piece by piece.

That is, unless I'm working a puzzle with my family. Then there's nothing joyful or serene about it. It's war!

> You find out a lot about the personalities of your family members when you sit down to work a puzzle together.

You find out a lot about the personalities of your family members when you sit down to work a puzzle together. Me? I'm an edger. I like to work the edge first. As a matter of fact, I have been known to start on the edge before all the pieces are out of the box and turned face up (a "personality disorder" that drives my daughter crazy).

But to me, the edge of the puzzle is crucial. You need to have the edge in place before you start any other step in the puzzle assembly. If you don't do the edge first, how will you know how much space you need on the table? How will you know what size frame to order? How will you know when you're going to have to cook supper again (because there's no way a puzzle that size is moving off the dining room table anytime soon)? There should be a rule—a law. You must work the edge first!

My daughter—my organized, firstborn, everything-in-its-place child—insists on getting all the pieces organized before we begin our puzzle working. She is adamant about the sky pieces. You must place them all face up around the top edge of the puzzle. Pieces with two prongs go on one line; pieces with an interlocking gap on all four sides go on the next line; then odd shapes; and so on, and so on. Reach across the table to grab a piece off the top row and allow your sleeve to mess up the neatly organized second row and . . . well, I can't promise that you'll return with all your fingers.

Then there is David, my husband. He's a picture studier. He picks out the object he wants to work in the picture on the puzzle box. Then he gathers all the pieces with the pertinent colors, shapes, and hues; scoops them into a cereal bowl; and moves to the end of the table away from the rest of the family. There he begins to work on his own private puzzle—alone. When he's done, he invariably turns to the rest of us and says in an obnoxious tone, "Got my part done. What's taking the rest of you so long? Hey, why don't you move the edge down here?"

"What? Move the edge?"

"Dad, you messed up my line!"

Before you know it, all joy is gone, and serenity falls by the wayside. Who would have thought that puzzle working could turn into a contact sport?

My mom is a funny puzzler. She's developed her own unique system—mainly, she says, because her eyesight is not so good; but I think it's because she doesn't want to fill up her table with puzzle pieces, just in case someone pops in for dinner. (I keep telling her that a nice thick table cloth will cover a puzzle quite adequately.) What's her method? Well, she does start with the edge. (She was a good teacher!) But she leaves all the pieces in the box. Then she picks them out one by one, twisting and turning each piece a dozen ways over every empty spot to see if it might fit. Never mind whether or not the colors match. It's all about finding a home for the one piece in her hand! When she has exhausted every possible empty spot, she places that piece in the box lid and moves on to another piece. It's crazy, if you ask me.

But Mom seems to really enjoy her puzzle. She's been working on the same one for the last four years.

Zachary, my son, is perhaps the smartest puzzler of us all. Or at least he is the most contrary! Just as the rest of us are picking up a good pace with our puzzling—the pieces are all out on the table, face up, organized, and slipping together nicely—Zachary emerges from his room long enough to come downstairs, stand nonchalantly by the table, slip a couple of pieces into his pocket, and then zip back up to his room. And there, he waits.

He waits until his mother is screaming at the top of her lungs: "Somebody, grab the dog!" He waits until every couch cushion has been turned upside down and thrown on the floor. He waits until I threaten to pump the dog's stomach again. And then—finally—he comes out of his room and taunts, "Look what I have. The last piece!"

That's what makes Zachary so smart when it comes to puzzles. He knows the one truth, the one basic premise that underlies all great puzzle work: The most important piece of the puzzle is always the last piece. Always.

A Glorious Mystery

Over the last eighteen months of my struggle with depression, I went through about fourteen Thomas Kincaid puzzles, a couple of mystery picture puzzles, and two 3-D puzzles that wound up looking like the ruins at Beit Shan in Israel. Puzzle working kept my mind occupied enough to forget I was depressed, and it was relaxing enough to not put too much strain on my few remaining brain cells. I found myself escaping into a dozen different landscapes and sailing away on a dozen different boats into a dozen different seas. I visited several Norman Rockwell neighborhoods, was a guest at a few murder-mystery tea parties, and surveyed the skylines of three major cities in the United States before it finally dawned on me: God is a puzzler.

In fact, he's the Master Puzzler, and he's been working the same puzzle since time began. Think about it. We are all pieces of an intricate landscape that was formed in his heart and mind and placed in a box on his dinner table. Slowly over time he has been putting us together, piece by interlocking piece. Colossians 1:17 says, "He is before all things, and in him all things hold together." If that's not proof that God's a great puzzler, I don't know what is!

What will the final picture look like? Well, that's the beautiful mystery of it all! The pieces of our lives come in a million shapes and sizes, colors and hues. The Master Puzzler carefully plucks each one from the box, examines it, and places it just where it needs to be. Colossians 1:27

says it like this, "God has chosen to make known . . . the glorious riches of this mystery."

When I was depressed, of course, the puzzle of my life seemed anything but glorious. It was gray. Colorless. Out of focus. Even Thomas Kincaid would have had trouble finding light in the darkness of such a landscape.

What kind of puzzler are you? Maybe you're the type who tries to force each piece to fit where you want it, when you want it. Piece by piece, twisting, turning, prodding—you're determined to do it your own way. You think, I know exactly what the final picture on the table should look like and how and when it should come together. No need to study the box, no need to organize the colors. I'll get this thing whipped into shape!

Or maybe you're the loner type. You gather the pieces you think you're going to need and then hunker down at the end of the table, away from everyone else. Somehow you feel safe there. You don't have to be bothered by input. You don't have to coordinate with other puzzlers. You can simply work on your own part of the puzzle—alone. Sure, you may feel a sense of accomplishment when you're done, but what happens when it's time to interlock with the rest of the world? You think, I don't fit in. I'm not ready for the world—or maybe the world isn't ready for me.

Perhaps you're an organizer. You have a plan. You've

done all the preparation. You've put all the pieces in rows, and everything is in perfect order. But then you get a phone call, and suddenly you find out you have breast cancer. Or you lose your job. Or you lose the drive to do your job. Engulfed in depression, you sit and stare at the big empty space on your dining room table, thinking, If there's a picture there somewhere, I'm sure I'm not in it.

Did you hear that? It's the missing piece! The heart is at the root of things.

Take heart, my fellow puzzle worker! God is the Master Puzzler. There is no second-guessing any piece of the puzzle when he is the one putting the picture together. He can organize the colors better than anyone (Have you seen a sunset lately?). He knows where to fit every shape and size (Have you seen a mountain range?). He can even pull a piece out of the center of the box—face down—and find the perfect spot for it every time. He never misses.

And one thing I know for a fact: He's an edger! Yes, God works the edge first. Think about it: the Ten Commandments, the Golden Rule, all the beautiful descriptions of holy living—they're in God's Word, the Bible, to help us place a boundary around our lives. Not to stifle our creativity or fence us in, but to give us an edge—to bring order to the chaos our world would otherwise be. With our edge in place, our lives have both definition and purpose.

I am learning every day to allow God to direct the pieces of my puzzle. I am learning to relax and believe that his plan—his picture for me—is better than anything I could imagine for myself. And when something happens, and my pieces get mixed up, tossed around, or turned upside down, I am learning to allow him to put things back in order. He can do it so much better than I can. The Message Bible puts it this way, in God's words: "The heart is hopelessly dark and deceitful, a puzzle that no one can figure out. But I, God, search the heart and examine the mind. I get to the heart of the human. I get to the root of things. I treat them as they are, not as they pretend to be" (Jeremiah 17:9–10).

Did you hear that? Can you see it? It's the missing piece! The heart is at the root of things.

It's the piece that was missing when I was deep in depression. Back then I searched, I questioned, I prodded. I was consumed with the effort to find it—that one last piece that would finally make sense of everything. But my mind was a dark, muddy mess, and I could barely think in the fog. When the medicine finally kicked in, my thoughts were less scrambled. But I still had unanswered questions: "Will it come back?" "Why can't I find peace of mind?" "Has God left me here alone?" I went back to work, but everywhere I went, I carried the same suitcase of nagging questions.

Then I came across Jeremiah 17, and it was as if the final puzzle piece started glowing right in front of me: "But I, God, search the heart and examine the mind. I get to the heart of the human."

You see, God has examined my mind. And yes, it has been a mess up there at times. He knows that; he is well aware of the crippling ordeal I've been through. But all along he has known that depression is only temporary. What has mattered most to him is getting to my heart.

Because, in the big picture of my life, my relationship with God has never been rooted in the confines of my frail mind. No, my relationship with him—like my relationships with all the really important people in my life—has always been rooted in my heart. And God knows my heart! He knows that the cry of my heart is Jeremiah 17:14: "God, pick up the pieces. Put me back together again. You are my praise!" (MSG).

Finishing the Puzzle

You know which puzzler in my house reminds me the most of God? My son, Zachary. He holds on to the last, most important piece until just the right time. Then he bounces down the steps like a victor, dances a goofy moon walk around the table, and sings, "Oh yeah! I'm good! I'm good!" (A bit obnoxious, I know. But it's almost impossible to remain aggravated at him; he's just so stinkin' cute.)

I know you can see it coming, but I'm going to point it out anyway: God holds the last piece! And I'm not just talking about the last piece of your particular puzzle. That's a given; he's held the picture of your life in pieces in his hands since the beginning of time. Matthew 10:30 says, "And even the very hairs of your head are numbered." Sounds like he can handle all your pieces, don't you think?

But God is not only holding your last piece; he's holding the last piece—the very last piece that finishes all he started in the Garden of Eden. The Master Puzzler has been actively working from the first piece he set on the table in Genesis to the piece he just put in place today. Soon he will gather the angels around him and announce, "Watch this!" Then, who knows? Maybe he will bounce around the table, do some kind of moon-walk dance, and shout, "You're good! You're good! Well done! Well done!"

And when that final piece is placed in the last empty spot, the sky will split wide open, and all our questions, concerns, and struggles with depression won't matter anymore. The picture will be complete.

The puzzle will be finished.

CHONDA'S INBOX

To: **Chonda**
Subject: **You are a blessing**
From: **Vicky**

Hi Chonda!

I took a friend with me to your show last night, and we enjoyed it so much. I didn't know that you have been struggling with depression. I'm so grateful that you shared about it! I have been dealing with depression all my life but wasn't diagnosed until recently. I, too, love working puzzles, and that helped me a lot during one particular episode (the most dreadful, awful, darkest, scariest time of my life). You are a blessing. Thank you so much for doing what you do!

Vicky

expert
insight

Hope for the Future

According to the National Institute of Mental Health (NIMH), 20 percent of American adults will suffer from a diagnosable mental disorder in a given year. Women will face these illnesses twice as often as men.

Unfortunately, many of these individuals will not seek help.

In an article written for Focus on the Family, Carolyn MacInnes notes, "Stigmas and misconceptions often prevent those with depressive illnesses (which often include anxiety and panic) from getting treatment. For some, words like mental illness and therapy still evoke images of patients in strait jackets or neurotic movie characters with phobias of germs, elevators, and their shadows. In reality, depression can be much less obvious. Even so, it still debilitates and destroys its victims if left untreated."[1]

If you're depressed, don't ignore it. Don't waste time feeling guilty. Don't worry about what other people will say or think. Get educated—and get help! Start with your internist or family doctor. Talk to your pastor. Find a professional counselor. Clinical depression is real, and it can be debilitating. But it also can be treated effectively. There is hope for the future—your future. Believe it!

epilogue

Put action to your faith, not your
feelings, and keep moving.

—Chonda Pierce

Arise from the depression and

prostration in which circumstances

have kept you—rise to a new life!
Shine, for your light
has come, and the glory of

the Lord has risen upon you!

—Isaiah 60:1

i'm back!

Well, I did it—headed back to work, that is. Real work, and not the one or two dates here and there that I've been enjoying for the last year or so. This time we routed a tour. Cities linked together with no more than five hundred miles between them, so we can drive there overnight by bus. Go to sleep in one city, wake up in the next. Church buildings, theaters, civic halls, auditoriums. Lots and lots of people—many who are willing to wait in line a long time after a show to tell me stories about their lives. Stories that sound a lot like my own.

I've lost track of the calendar. Can't tell you what day of the week it is, or even what time. Ah, the perils of changing time zones! I have to ask the driver what town we're in. If his answer doesn't ring a bell, I follow up with, "What state?"

The other day I was sitting on the bus in Seattle, Washington, one hand resting on my make-up case. By my count we were on our twelfth day away from home. The bus had lost its new-bus smell days earlier and had taken on a new odor: that of an old garbage truck at the end of its route. I lifted the window shade to see rain drizzling off the glass. So what else is new? I'm pretty sure that Seattle is a Native American word for "rains every day."

I angled the mirror on the table in front of me and began the all-too-familiar routine of fixing my face before heading into the concert venue to make a couple thousand women laugh. I noticed a few lines at the corners of my eyes that hadn't been there two weeks earlier. Nothing a little more foundation can't take care of, I figured.

I emptied all the tiny tubes, bottles, and jars from my make-up case onto the table, finished my make-up, and turned to push the ON button of the coffee pot. Then I tugged on my socks and my really nice shoes—the ones I only wear on stage because they're so uncomfortable. I shook my head (and newly painted face) and wondered, Will anyone notice that I've been wearing the same socks for three days? But then, how could they, unless I tell them? And I would never, ever do that on stage—or in a book, for that matter.

Somewhere between applying my blush and sipping my French Vanilla Folger's, it dawned on me: I'm here—on tour. This has been a long run. And . . . I'm fine! Oh, I'm definitely stretched and stressed. My shoulders are sagging a bit. But I'm not depressed.

Wow! I'm back!

About that time my road manager, Matt, stuck his head in the bus door and said, "Hey, I got a call today from Women of Faith. They want you to come and speak at their national conference in San Antonio, Texas. Remember that place? Satan's hotel?" He paused to allow me to conjure up the dark memories. The last time I was there, I was deeply depressed. It was in a hotel in San Antonio that I first heard the talking lights.

"Wanna give it a try?" he asked.

I took a deep breath and thought about my response. Then I realized I could have thought about it without taking such a deep breath (garbage truck, remember?). I grinned, wiggled my toes as much as my really nice, uncomfortable shoes would allow, and said, "Yeah. Let's do it."

He gave me one of those kinds of nods that the

managers at NASA always give the astronauts just before launch—one loaded with professionalism, empathy, and, I think, something like admiration.

"Good," he said. "I'll make the call."

It was time to go, so I scooped up a tube of lipstick and tucked it in my pocket. Then I followed my road manager down the bus steps and into the auditorium, just as someone announced my name and handed me a microphone. But before I switched it on so the whole auditorium could hear me, I leaned over to Matt and whispered, "Do you remember the name of the hotel we stayed in last time we were in San Antonio?"

Even in the dim light of backstage, I could see his nod.

"Great. Let's stay somewhere else this time—just in case. Someplace where the lights don't talk."

Then I switched on the microphone and stepped into the warm spotlight. I was tired, but I still felt like making some people laugh.

It's good to be back.

notes

chapter 7 : are we there yet?

1. Robert J. Morgan, The Red Sea Rules: The Same God Who Led You In Will Lead You Out (Nashville: Thomas Nelson Publishers, 2001), 9.

2. Matthew Henry, "Complete Commentary on Mark 6," Matthew Henry's Complete Commentary on the Whole Bible (1706, public domain), http://www.studylight.org/com/mhc-com/view.cgi?book=mr&chapter=006.

chapter 8 : enough baloney

1. Beth Moore, Breaking Free: Making Liberty in Christ a Reality in Life (Nashville: Broadman and Holman Publishers, 2000), 117.

2. Ibid.

231

chapter 10: maintain, maintain, maintain!

1. Gerald Beals, "Thomas Edison Quotes," Copyright 1996. All rights reserved. http://www.thomasedison.com/edquote.htm.

2. Derek Prince, Blessings and Curses (Grand Rapids: Baker Publishing Group, 2003).

chapter 11: the master puzzler

1. Carolyn MacInnes, "How to Help When Your Spouse Is Depressed," Focus on the Family, copyright 2006, all rights reserved, at http://www.family.org/married/comm/a0027675.cfm.